The Curial
made by maystere Alain Charretier

EARLY ENGLISH TEXT SOCIETY

Extra Series, No. 54

1888 (reprinted 1965)

Price 10s.

DEDICATED TO
MY FRIEND AND HELPER
F. S. ELLIS

F. J. F.

The Curial

made by maystere Alain Charretier

Translated thus in Englyssh by

William Caxton

1484

COLLATED WITH THE FRENCH ORIGINAL
BY
PAUL MEYER

AND EDITED BY
FREDERICK J. FURNIVALL

Published for
THE EARLY ENGLISH TEXT SOCIETY
by the
OXFORD UNIVERSITY PRESS
LONDON   NEW YORK   TORONTO

OXFORD
UNIVERSITY PRESS

Great Clarendon Street, Oxford OX2 6DP
United Kingdom

Oxford University Press is a department of the University of Oxford.
It furthers the University's objective of excellence in research, scholarship,
and education by publishing worldwide. Oxford is a registered trade mark of
Oxford University Press in the UK and in certain other countries

© The Early English Text Society 1888

The moral rights of the authors have been asserted

Database right Oxford University Press (maker)

First Edition published in 1888
Reprinted 1935, 1965

All rights reserved. No part of this publication may be reproduced,
stored in a retrieval system, or transmitted, in any form or by any means,
without the prior permission in writing of Oxford University Press,
or as expressly permitted by law, or under terms agreed with the appropriate
reprographics rights organization. Enquiries concerning reproduction
outside the scope of the above should be sent to the Rights Department,
Oxford University Press, at the address above

You must not circulate this book in any other form
and you must impose this same condition on any acquirer

Published in the United States of America by Oxford University Press
198 Madison Avenue, New York, NY 10016, United States of America

British Library Cataloguing in Publication Data
Data available

Library of Congress Cataloging in Publication Data
Data available

Extra Series, 54

ISBN 978-0-19-722516-5

FOREWORDS.

OF this book printed by Caxton in 1484 (no doubt), in his type No. 4*, Mr. Blades says, in his *Biography and Typography of William Caxton*, 2nd edition, 1882, p. 297 :—

"Caxton translated the Curial from the French 'for a noble and virtuous Erle,' probably Lord Rivers, who was beheaded at Pomfret, on June 13th, 1483.

"Alain Chartier, born in Normandy about 1386, earned for himself the appellation of 'excellent orateur, noble poëte, et très-renommé rhétoricien.' He held the office of 'Secretaire de la Maison' to both Charles VI and Charles VII. He died about 1457. The most complete editions of his works are those by Galiot du Pré, 16mo, Paris, 1529; and by Duchesne, 4to, Paris, 1617. In the former, however, is an error which has led to some confusion, as 'Livre de l'Esperance' is there entitled 'Le Curial,' the real Curial being a much shorter piece, and totally different in design. By the 'Curial' being addressed to his brother, it is supposed to have been written by Alain to Jean Chartier, known as the author of 'Histoire de Charles VII.'

"As an instance of the great repute in which the writings of Chartier were held in his age, it is reported that Margaret, the wife of the Dauphin of France, afterwards Louis XI, finding him one day asleep in his chair, kissed his lips, to the great astonishment of her attendants. 'Je ne baise pas la personne, mais la bouche dont estoient sortés tant de beaux discours,' she exclaimed. There is a painting in Add. MS. No. 15,300 (in the British Museum) vividly depicting this scene."

The above statement about the Dauphiness kissing Alain Chartier, is left as Mr. Blades wrote it; but he cannot have seen the one illumination in the Addit. MS. 15,300. That pictures a big-headed crownd lady standing up with her arms spread, as if in astonishment, with a stout man lying on the ground before her, possibly asleep,— his left hand covers part of his face,—while at her left is an armd man leaning on a 2-handed sword; and on his left, a seated scribe writing. In the background is the city wall, with a turreted gate, and towerd and turreted buildings inside. The MS is one of Alain Chartier's *Quadrilogus Invectivus*, written because he thought the hand of God was upon France, inasmuch as "en l'an mil CCCC, vint et deux, Ie veisse le Roy anglois, ancien aduersaire de ceste seigneurie, soy glorifier en no*st*re ignominieux reproche, Enrichir de noz despoilles, et desprisier noz faiz et noz courages" (leaf 5, back). (lf. 6) " Et Ie, meu de compassion pour ramener a memoire l'estat de no*st*re infelicite, & a chascun ramenteuoir ce que lui en touche, Ay composé ce present traictie q*ue* l'appelle [*lf.* 6, *bk.*] 'quadrilogue', pource que, en quatre perso*n*nages est ceste euure comprise. Et est dit 'Inuectif', en tant qu'il procede par maniere d'enuaisseme*n*t de paroles, et par forme de reprandre."

Of the *Curial*, says Mr. Blades, only two copies are known; one is in the British Museum (here reprinted), and the other at Althorpe, Lord Spencer's Library. The Collation is

" A 3^{n1}, signed j, ij, iij, without any blanks: In all, six leaves. There is no title-page. The type is entirely No. 4*. The lines, which are spaced to an even length, measure $4\frac{7}{8}$ inches, and there are 38 to a full page. Without catchwords or folios. The Text begins on sig. .j. recto ... The 'Curial' finishes on the sixth recto ... On the verso, Caxton has given us the translation of a ballad, written by Alain Chartier, consisting of 28 lines. It has a burthen :—' Ne chyer but of a man Joyous.'"

In itself, the *Curial* or Letter has little literary worth; but Caxton englisht it, and that fact justifies its reprint. Moreover, short books are always handy for the E. E. T. Soc. The subject is the old one which afterwards interested Shakspere;—compare the Duke, Touchstone &c. in *As You Like It*, and Belisarius in *Cymbeline*, III. iii.;—the disadvantages of the intriguing restless life at Court, compared with the quiet and restfulness of the country. Two books on this topic which are well worth reading, were reprinted by Mr. W. C. Hazlitt in his *Roxburghe Library*, 1868 :

---

[1] A *Ternion* is 6 leaves, 12 pages. A 4^n is a *Quaternion*, 8 leaves. A 5^n or *Quinternion*, is a section of 5 sheets folded together in half, making 10 leaves or 20 pages.—*ib*, p. 168.

1. *Cyuile and Vncyuile Life*, as its headlines call it, tho' the full title is

"The English / Courtier, and the / Cu*n*trey-gentleman : / A pleasaunt and learned Disputation, / betweene them both : very profitable and ne- / cessarie to be read of all Nobilitie / and Gentlemen / Wherein is discoursed, vvhat / order of lyfe, best beseemeth a Gentleman, (aswell for e- / ducation, as the course of his whole life) to make him a / person fytte for the publique seruice of his Prince and / Countrey. / Imprinted at London, by / Richard Iones : dwelling at the signe / of the Rose and Crowne neere / vnto Holborne Bridge. 1586. / An earlier Qto. 1579.

2. [by Nicholas Breton.] The / Court and Country, / or / A Briefe Discourse betweene the / Courtier and Country-man ; / of the Manner, Nature, and Condi- / tion of their liues. / Dialogue-wise set downe betwixt a / Courtier and Country-man. / Conteyning many Delectable and Pithy / Sayings, worthy Observation. / Also, necessary Notes for a Covrtier. / Written by N. B. Gent. / London / Printed by G. Eld for Iohn Wright, and are to / be Sold at his Shoppe at the Signe of the Bible / without Newgate. / 1618. /

Alain Chartier's sketch of the French courtier of his time is not a cheering one. But it differs little from those of the English Elizabethan courtier by Spenser in his *Colin Clowt*, and by Harrison in his *Description of England*.

Both were the necessary consequence of despots being the sole sources of honour, and their whims being law. And though Society and Fashion still breed Flunkeyism and Falseness, and some Demagogs pander to the base prejudices of all classes from the highest to the lowest, we may surely believe that our Victorian time is better, in this regard, than the Caroline in France, or the Elizabethan here.

The headlines, side-notes, and modern stops of the Text are mine. Caxton's tagd *d* and *g* are not reproduced.

July, 1888.

P.S. Oct. 1888. My chance sending of a proof to my old friend Prof. Paul Meyer, induced him, in the kindest possible way, to set aside all his own pressing work, and not only collate for us Caxton's English with the French original, and give us many most valuable corrections and explanations of Caxton's text—see the footnotes,— but also to hunt out and copy for us the original of the supposed

Balade by Alain Chartier which Caxton englisht and printed at the end of his *Curial*. Prof. P. Meyer has also written an Introduction to the Balade, which will be found on p. 17 below, and the following comments on Alain Chartier's *Curial*, and Caxton's englishing of it.

All our Members will join with me in thanking Prof. Meyer for his great kindness, and his admirable enrichment of the present little Text.

COMMENT BY PROF. P. MEYER.

The French *Curial* has been printed several times since the first edition of Alain Chartier's works (Paris, Le Caron, 1489), until Du Chesne's much improved edition (Paris, 1617).[1] The manuscripts are not scarce, but those which I have seen are very corrupt. So are, and even worse, the ancient editions, previous to Du Chesne. Chartier writes, particularly in his *Curial*, a refined and elaborate style which has often been misunderstood by the copyists. We must not wonder if Caxton's translation is not free from mistakes. Some of these are to be traced to the MS. which he used, some to mere misreadings, some to excusable misunderstandings. A due allowance being made for the difficulties of the task, the translation cannot be pronounced to be wanting in force and intelligence. One noticeable peculiarity in Caxton's anglicizing of the *Curial* is the habit of rendering some of the words of the original by two consecutive synonyms,[2] one of them being the very word of Chartier, the other a more generally accepted English word. For example, p. 5, l. 19, "ewrous and happy," for the Fr. *heureux*; l. 23, "rendre and yelde," for the Fr. *rendre*; p. 7, l. 22, "the dore . . . of the chambre or wythdraught," Fr. *l'uys du retrait*; p. 8, l. 21, "the ryghtes and droytes," Fr. *les droits*; p. 9, l. 27, "rendrid and gafe," Fr. *rendoient*, etc.

Whenever Caxton's translation has been found defective or erroneous, the French text has been quoted from Du Chesne's edition; the MSS. having been resorted to only in special cases.—P. M.

---

[1] For a full description of the editions, see Brunet, *Manuel du libraire*, under CHARTIER (*Alain*).

[2] This practice is known also in the English Bible and Prayer-book.—F.J.F.

[The Curial of Alain Charretier.]

⁴ Here foloweth the copye of a lettre whyche maistre Alayn Charetier wrote to hys brother / whyche desired to come dwelle in Court / in whyche he reherseth many myseryes & wretchydnesses therin vsed[1] / For taduyse
⁸ hym not to entre in to it / leste he after repente / like as hier after folowe / and late translated out of frensshe in to englysshe / whyche Copye was delyuerid to me by a noble and vertuous Erle / At whos Instance &
¹² requeste I haue reduced it in to Englyssh.

Yght welbelouyd brother, & persone Eloquent / thou admonestest and exhortest me to prepare & make redy, place and entree for the vnto the lyf
¹⁶ Curiall / whyche thou desirest / And that by my helpe and requeste thou myghtest haue therin offyce / And herto thou art duly[2] meuyd by comyn errour of the people / whiche repute thonours mondayne & pompes of
²⁰ them of the courte / to be thynges more blessyd & happy than other / or to thende that I Iuge not wel[3] of thy desyre / Thou wenest parauenture / that they that wayte on offices / ben in vertuous occupacions, & reputest them
²⁴ the more worthy for to haue rewardes & merites / And also thou adioustest other causes that meue the therto /

[sign. j.]
The Letter that Alain Chartier wrote to dissuade his Brother from coming to Court. Englisht by Wm. Caxton.

Dear Brother, you ask me to get you a place at Court,

thinking that men in office are virtuous,

---

[1] Nearly every final d is ď in the original, and every final g has a like curl to it.

[2] French *indeuement*, but the MS. used by Caxton may have had *deuement*.—P. M.

[3] The French has: "ou afin que je ne juge *mal* de ton desir."—P. M.

2   The daily Dangers and Miseries of Life at Court.

<small>and that you will be in the company of me,</small>

<small>your old friend.</small>

<small>I too long for you.</small>

<small>But when I suffer daily in the public service,</small>

<small>I feel happy that you escape my troubles at Court.</small>

<small>[* sign. j. back]</small>

<small>You want to be with me at Court. I wish more to be alone with you.</small>

by thexample of me / that empesshe my selue for to serue in the courte Ryall / And to thende that thou myghtest vse thy dayes in takyng companye wyth me / and that we myghte to-gidre enioye the swettenes of frendshyppe / whyche longe tyme hath ben bytwene vs tweyne / And thys knowe I wel / that thy courage is not wythdrawen fer from my frendshyppe / And the grace of humanyte is not dreyed vp in the / whyche compryseth hys frendes as presente, And leueth not at nede to counseylle & ayde them absente to hys power / And I trowe that thyn absence is not lasse greuous to me / than myn is to thy self / For me semeth, that thou beyng absente, I am there where the places and affayres desioyne vs / But by cause god of fortune hath so departed our destynee / that thou awaytest frely on thyn owne pryuate thynges / And that I am occupyed on thynges publycque, & seruyses in sorowful passions / that whan I haue on my self compassion / Thenne am I enioyed of thyn ease / & take grete playsir / in this, that *tho*u auoydest the myserries that I suffre euery day / And yf I blame or accuse fortune for me / I preyse and thanke her on that other parte for the / For so moche as she hath exempte the fro the anguysshes that I suffre *in the courte / And that she hath not made vs bothe meschaunte /

Thou desirest, as thou sayst, to be in the courte wyth me / And I coueyte yet more to be pryuely and syngulerly wyth the / And also for me thou woldest gladly leue thy fraunchyse and pryuate lyf / I ought more gladly for the loue of the, leue thys seruytude mortell / For as moche as loue acquyteth hym better in humble tranqullyte than in orguyllous myserye / late hyt suffyse to the & to me / that one of vs tweyne be Infortunat / And that by my meschaunte lyf thou mayst see and knowe more certaynly that one and that other fortune / But what demaundest thou / Thou sechest the way to lese thy

4

8

12

16

20

24

28

32

36

Keep away from Court! It is full of Liars and Ill-doers. 3

self / by thexample of me / And wylt lepe fro the *Why will you jump from the Haven of Security into the Sea of Misery?*
hauen of sewerte / for to drowne thy self in the see
of peryl and myserye / Repentest thou the to haue
4 lyberte / Art thou annoyed to lyue in peas / humayne *Human Nature always longs for what it hasn't.*
nature hath suffred suche vnhappynes / that she ap-
petyteth and desireth to haue that thyng / whyche she
hath not / Thus misprysest thou the peas of thy corage /
8 and the sure estate of thy thought / And by therrour
of mésprysement whyche thou hast goten / the thynges
whyche of theyr owne condicion ben more to be mes-
prised / than they that ben shewde by the lyf of
12 another[1] / I meruaylle me moche / how thou, that art
prudent and wyse of goodes[2] / art so ouerseen and fro
thy self, for to dar expose thy self to so many perillis.
And yf thou wylt vse my counseyl / Take none *But take my advice: Don't come to Court.*
16 example by me for to poursewe the courtes / Ne the
publycque murmures of hye palaysis / But alleway late
my perylle be example to the for to fle and eschewe
them / For I dar not afferme / that emonge the bruyt
20 of them that torne / be ony thyng stedfast ne hol-
somme / Thou shalt wene & hope to fynde / exercite of
vertu / in myserye thus commune & publycque / And
so certaynly shalt thou fynde / yf thou makest thy view[3]
24 to fight constauntly agenst alle vices / But be ware &
make good watche that thou be not the fyrst that shal
be ouercome / For I saye the / that the courtes of hye *Courts are full of deceivers, bullies, flatterers, hinderers of good.*
prynces be neuer disgarnysshed of peple deceyuyng by

---

[1] Caxton's phrase seems to be unfinished. The Fr. has: "Les choses qui de leur mesme condition (that is, on account of their very condition) sont plus a mespriser que par vices (var. *que par la vie,* Caxton's reading) d'autruy a priser, *tu loues et exauces.*" The last words, "thou praisest and exaltest," seem to have been left out.—P. M.

[2] *of goods* has no meaning. The French has: " . . . qui es prudent et saige *deviens* si forsené." Caxton may have misread *de biens* instead of *deviens,* becomest.—P. M.

[3] Caxton's *view* is a mistake for *vow,* Fr. *veu:* "se tu fais veu de batailler," if thou vowest, or takest a pledge, to be constantly fighting.—P. M.

4   *No Courtier succeeds who is not corruptible.*

fayr langage / or feryng by menaces / or stryuyng by enuye / or corrupte by force of yeftes / or blandysshyng by flaterers / or accusyng of trespaces / or enpesshyng & lettyng in somme maner wyse / the good wyl of true men ; For our poure humanyte is lyghtly enclyned to ensiewe & folowe[1] the maners & condycions of other / And to doo as they doo. *And vnnethe may he escape that is asseged and assaylled of so many aduersaryes / Now late vs graunte that thou woldest perseuere in vertue / And that thou sholdest escape the vycyous and the corrupcion of suche vycyous persones / yet in thys caas thou haddest vaynquysshed none but thy self / But thys had ben better that thou haddest don it in thy owne secrete pryue place. And be thou certayn, that for thy vertue thou shalt be mocqued, and for thy trouthe thou shalt be hated / or that thy dyscrecion shal cause the to be suspecte / For ther is nothyng more suspecte to euyl peple / than them whom they knowe to be wyse and trewe /

The reste thenne is thys / that thou shalt haue labour wythoute fruyt / And shalt vse thy lyf in perylle / And shalt gete many enuyous at the / And yf thou stryue at theyr enuye / or that thou takest vengeance / I telle to the, that thy vengement shal engendre to the, more greuous aduersytees[2] than thou haddest tofore / And by the contrarye / they that conne dyssymyle, ben preysed, and vse better theyr tyme in courtes than the other peple / The abuses of the courte / And the maner of the peple curyall or courtly ben suche that a man is neuer suffred tenhaunce hym self / but yf he be corrumpable / For vertue whyche is in so many maners enuyed[3] / yf she be not prowde / she is mesprysed / yf she bowe not / she is by force sette abacke / yf she be broken or hurte, she is by force

---

Our poor humanity follows bad examples.

[* sign. ij.]

If you keep virtuous,

you'll be mockt and hated;

your life 'll be in danger,

and you'll be worse off than before.

Corruption is the only way to success at Court.

---

[1] *Orig.* folo-lowe   [2] Fr. *adversaires.*—P. M.
[3] Another mistake of Caxton's: the French is '*environnée.*'—P. M.

hunted away / who is he thenne that may kepe hym
that he be not corrupt or coromped / or who is he that
shall escape without hauyng harme / Suche be the
4 werkes of the courte, that they that be symple ben   *The simple are despised, the virtuous envied.*
mesprysed / the vertuous enuyed / And the prowde
arrogaunts in mortel peryllis / And yf thou be sette
doun and put aback vnder the other courtyours /
8 Thou shalt be enuyous of theyr power / yf thou be in
mene estate / of whyche thou hast not suffysaunce /
thou shalt stryue for to mounte and ryse hyer / And yf
thou mayst come vnto the hye secrets whyche ben
12 strongly for to doubte and drede / in the doubtous
courteynes of the most hye prynces / Thenne shalt thou
be most meschaunt / Of somoche as thou wenest to be   *When you seem most happy, and in high position,*
most ewrous¹ and happy / so moche more shalt thou be
16 in grete perill to falle / lyke to hym that is mounted in
to the most hye place / For to them whom fortune the
variable hath most hyely *lyfte up / and enhaunsed /   [* sign. ij. back]
resteth nomore but for to falle fro so hye doun / by   *then Fortune will ruin you*
20 cause she oweth to them nothyng but ruyne / yf thou
haste take of her alle that thou myghtest / and that
she wold gyue / thenne art thou debytour of thy self /
To thende that she rendre and yelde hym meschaunt   *and make you miserable.*
24 whom she had enhaunsed / And that she mocque hym
of hys meschef whom she had made blynde of vayn
glorye of hys enhaunsyng / For the grete wyndes that
blowe in hye courtes ben of suche condicion / that they
28 only that ben hyest enhaunsed / ben after theyr des-   *As soon as Courtiers reach the highest posts, they are envied and hated till they are abased.*
poyntement / as a spectacle of enuye / of detraction /
or of hate vnto alle peple / and fynde them self sub-
gettes tyl they be shamed and put doun emong the
32 peple² / And that they that tofore poursiewed to them
and flatered / Reporte of them more gretter blames and
dyvysions³ than the other / For multytude of peple

---

¹ Fr. *eureux: heur* of *bonheur, malheur*
² Fr. "entre les populaires," viz. among the mob, low people.
—P. M.   ³ Misprint? Fr. *derisions.*—P. M.

6 The Fall of great Lords delights Fortune. Courtiers seek her.

<small>Fortune</small>

<small>laughs and claps her hands when great lords fall into trouble.</small>

<small>Men of high and whole hearts disregard Fortune.</small>

<small>The Court thinks too much of Fortune.</small>

<small>[* sign. iij.]</small>

mespryse alwaye them / that fortune hath most aualed[1] and throwen doun / And also is envyous of them that she seeth enhaunsed and lyft vp / Fortune gladly hath sette hys eyen on hem that ben in hye degree, and on the soueraynes yet more / And whan she pleyeth wyth smale and poure folkes / that is no certayn / for of the meschief of poure peple she retcheth not / ne doth but smyle / But she lawgheth wyth ful mouth, and smyteth her paulmes to gydre, whan she seeth grete lordes falle in to meschyef / she retcheth but lytel for tessaye and preue her fortune in lytyl and lowe places / But for to make the grete and myghty to falle and ouerthrowe, she setteth gladly her gynnes / And them that ben poure & caste doun, maketh she oftymes to ryse & mounte fro certaynte to Incertaynte, and fro good rewle to euyl rewle / Them deceyueth she gladly / whom she fyndeth esy to deceyue / and variable as she is / But she doth the custommes & strength to them that setteth by her.[2] And whan she seeth her despysed & nought sette by / thenne she leueth them in peas / But she flateryth and lawgheth for nought vnto them that haue hye and hole courage / Now she essayeth to Iuste ayenst them that ben most stronge / And now she enhaunseth the*m* that ben most feble / now she lawheth to one / and she grymmeth to other / But the man that hath grete corage & vertuous, mespriseth her lawhynges and mowes / And nothyng doubteth her menaces / [3]But the courte maketh ouer moche compte of thys fortune / that draweth the peple lyghtly to her / *forgetyng theyr poure estate / And forgetyng

4

8

12

16

20

24

28

---

[1] From *à val;* orig. Fr. *ravallés*, cast down.—P. M.

[2] What does this mean? The French has (in MS. texts, for Du Chesne's edition is corrupt here) : "Mais elle *hait* les constans et vertueulx qui elle ne font compte." Caxton seems to have read "Mais elle *fait* les coustumes."—P. M.

[3-3] This passage was completely misunderstood by Caxton. He ought to have translated "maketh moche more compte of thys fortune . . . *than* she doth of the wyse men." French :

and not knowyng them self as sone as they ben en-
haunced / whyche the wyse men do not / whiche for *But wise men rest content.*
none auauncement ne hauyng of good, enpayre not them
4 self³ / There assaye thou for to mounte / yf thou wylt
leue thy lyberte and franchyse / Thenne oughtest thou
to knowe / that thou shalt haue habundaunce thy self /
whan thou shalt wylle to poursewe the court / whyche
8 maketh a man to leue hys propre maners / And to applye *The Court makes you give up your*
hym self to the maners of other. For yf he be veryt- *own morals for worse ones,*
able / men shal holde hym atte scole of fayntyse / yf
he loue honest lyf / men shal teche hym to lede dys-
12 honest lyf / yf he be pacyent / & sette by no prouffyt¹ /
he shal be left to haue suffraunce / For yf he can
nought / men shal demau*n*de him nothyng / And also
he shal fynde none / that shal gyue hym ony thyng² /
16 yf he entre Inportunatly / They that be Inportune shal
put hym abacke / yf he be acustomed to ete soberly / *and your own habits for other*
and at a certayn houre / he shal dyne late, and shal *folk's.*
soupe in suche faco*u*n that he shal disacustom*m*e hys
20 tyme and hys maner of lyuyng / Yf he haue be
acustomed to rede and studye in bookes / he shal muse *At Court, the Student must*
ydelly alday, in awaytyng that men shal open the dore *turn Idler and Place-hunter.*
to hym, of the chambre or wythdraught of the prynce /
24 yf he loue the rest of his body, he shal be ennoyed³
now here / nowe there / as a courrour or renner per-
petuell / yf he wil erly goo to his bedde, and Ryse late
at his playsir, he shal faylle therof / For he shal wake
28 longe and late / and ryse ryght erly / and that ofte he

"Mais la court fait trop plus grant compte de celle fortune . .
. . . . . qu'elle ne fait des (*ed.* les) sages qui, pour bien avoir,
ne se empirent."—P. M.
¹ Fr. "Et non chalant d'avoir prouffit," viz. "and cares
not to have profit."—P. M.
² Mistranslation arising from a bad text. Fr. "S'il ne
sçait ou ne veut riens demander, aussi ne trouvera il qui riens
luy donne."—P. M.
³ Unless Caxton printed "*ennoyed*" for *enuoyed*, envoyed,
he must have read *ennuyé;* but the French has *envoyé*, sent
on an errand.—P. M.

C

8 *The dependence of Court life: the independence of Country life.*

<small>Every one must lose his natural rest,</small>

shal lese the nyght wythout slepyng / yf he studye for to fynde frendshyp / he[1] shal neuer conne[2] trotte so moche thurgh the halles of the grete lordes that he

<small>and yet not gain favour.</small>

shal fynde her / but she holdeth her wythoute, and entreth not wyth ony / For she is moche better knowen by them that vsen her, whyche ben experte of reffuse /[3] throwen doun by fortune / than by them that entre ygnoraunt / and not knowen her tornes / Now beholde thenne / and see, whyche of the two thou shalt chese / or that in my yssuyng and goyng out / I drawe the to our comune prouffyt, or in thyn entryng thou brynge me to our comune dommage and hurte / And forgete

<small>The Courtier is always lodgd in another's house,</small>

not that who serueth in the courte / Alway hym behoueth to be a gheste / and herberowed in another

<small>and must eat, and sleep at another's will.</small>

mannes hows / And also he muste ete after thappetyte of other / and otherwhyle wythoute hungre, and fayn he maye / And in lyke wyse he muste wake otherwhyle

<small>[* sign. iij. back]</small>

atte *the wylle of other / after that he hath begonne to slepe, and by grete gryef,[4] what thyng is more domageus than to sette vnder fortune the vertues of nature / and the ryghtes and droytes of lyf humayne / seen that it is [not][5] a thyng more free in a man / than to lyue naturelly. emong vs seruantes of courte / we doo nothynge but

<small>A country householder is a King in his own house.</small>

lyue after thordonance of other / And thou lyuest in thyn hous lyke an Emperour / thou regnest as a kyng paysyble / vnder the couuerte of thyn hous / And we tremble for drede to dysplayse the lordes of hye houses /

<small>Contrast the ills of the Court and the good of the Country, in eating,</small>

Thou mayst ete whan thou hast hungre / at thyn houre and at thy playsir / And we ete so gredyly & gloutonnously, that otherwhyle we caste it vp agayn

<small>sleeping,</small>

and make vomytes / Thou passest the nyght in slepyng

4

8

12

16

20

24

28

---

[1] *he* means friendship; Fr. "jamais elle ne scet troter."— P. M.

[2] be able to, know how to

[3] *reffuse* is evidently wrong. The French has "expers des ruses (ed. *jeux*) de fortune," its tricks.—P. M.

[4] Fr. "par grief sommeil," heavy sleep.—P. M.

[5] Fr. "veu qu'il *n*'est chose plus franche."—P. M.

Private Life is far better than Public Life in Courts. 9

as long as it playseth the / And we, after ouermoche
drynkyng of wynes and grete paynes, lye doun ofte in
beddes ful of vermyne / & somtyme wyth stryf and   *and beds.*
4 debate¹ /
 Retourne, brother / Retourne to thy self / And
lerne to know the felicite / by the myseryes that we   *Recognise the*
suffre / But no-man preyseth ynough the ayses that he   *happiness of private life.*
8 hath in his pryuate and propre hous / but he that to-
fore mespryseth thanguysshes that he hath suffred in
admynystracion publycque / Arystotle the phylosophre   *Neither Aristotle*
gloryfyed in hym self / that he had left the hye palays
12 of kyng Alysaundre / And had leuer to leue there hys
discyple Calistenes / than there lenger to dwelle /
Dyogenes also, whiche in hys tyme, aboue alle other   *nor Diogenes cared for courts*
men louyd lyberte and fraunchyse, Refused the grete   *or wealth.*
16 rychesses and wordly Ioyes to whyche he was callyd /
he fledde them for to enhabyte and dwelle frely wythin
the tonne / wherin he slepte / And also durst somoche
auau̇nte hym / that he was more puyssaunt prynce, in
20 that he myght more reffuse of goodes, than the said
Alysaundre hath power to gyue hym. For the veray
phylosophre / that can wel mespryse thambycious
vanyte of the peple of the court / techeth to his coun-
24 seyllours² / that ther is more of humanyte in smale   *There is more Humanity in*
thynges and eases³ / than in the courtes of prynces /   *private life than in Princes' courts.*
And the benes of Pictagoras / And the wortes that
Orace ete / rendrid and gafe better sauour / than that
28 Sardanapalus fonde in the grete and delycious wynes
Aromatyques that he dranke / for as moche as the
delyces were medled with the galle of poyson / Feures /
& anguysshes mondaynes / that he had alway vpon hys
32 herte / not only our lyf / but thexaction of our lyf /
hys tormentis adioyne to our lyf in suche wyse that

---

¹ Fr. "atout le bast," means harnessed, dressed.—P. M.
² French, "Car vraye *Philosophie* est quand on sçait mespriser . . . et apprendre a ses *escolliers*."—P. M.
³ French *cases*, poor houses, not *causes*.—P. M.

CURIAL.   B

10   *All is not Gold that glitters.   Courtiers seek Titles, not Right.*

[* leaf iiij.]

Folk think much of a Courtier's rich dress; but they don't know the cost and trouble of it.

Courtiers' deckings are not won by merit.

They think more of official titles than Right, and of Words than Things.

They desire Honour, tho' they know they arn't worthy of it.

*she ne hath glorye mondayne / ne pompe caduque wythoute aduersyte / Oftymes the peple make grete wondrynges of the Ryche robe of the courtyour[1] / but they knowe not by what labour ne by what dyffyculte 4 he hath goten it /

The peple otherwhyle honoureth and worshypeth the grete apparaylle of a puyssant man, But they acompte not the pryckkyng that he hath felte in the 8 pourchassyng of it / Ne the greuys that he hath goten in shewyng of yt / Othertymes beholde the peple thordynaunces and grete houshold of the hye and grete lordes / but they knowe not of what dyspence they ben 12 charged for to nourysshe them / Ne consydre nothyng the tytle / of whyche they knowe certaynly / that they haue in them no merites / Yf we calle an hare / a lyon / or saye that a fayr mayde is fowle[2] / or a fowle / croke- 16 backed / haltyng / or euyl shapen, to be as fayre as Helayne / that shold be a grete lesynge / and worthy of derysion / And allewaye emonge vs courtyours enfayned / we folowe more the names of thoffyces / than 20 the droytes and ryghtes / we be verbal / or ful of wordes / and desyre more the wordes than the thynges / And in thys we ben contrarye to the wyse Cathon / whyche desired more to excersise hym self vertuously 24 in comune offyce and publycque / than to haue the name / And in suche wyse gouerneth he hym self / that whan he was called / he was alleway founde worthy to haue better than he was callyd to / And 28 somoche more was he honowred / as whan he fledde most the worldly honours / But by the contrarye we coueyte to be honowred / how wel that we ben not worthy / And so take the honours as by force and 32

---

[1] French, "De la riche robe d'un pautonnier." Evidently Caxton did not understand *pautonnier*, a vagabond, a contemptible man.—P. M.

[2] French, "que une jeune fille laide, bossue, ou mal atournée, fust aussi belle comme Helene."—P. M.

strengthe / er we ben called therto. And herof foloweth
that we lese by good ryght / that whyche we Iuge[1] to
our self, and that we dar demande indewly / And to
4 saye trouthe, the honours flee fro vs / whyche we
poursewe ouer folyly /

Therefore, brother, I counseylle the / that thou *So, Brother,*
delyte the / in thy self / of thy vertue / For she
8 yeldeth Ioye and preysynge to them that lyue wel /
late thy grete suffysaunce[2] reteyne the wythin thy lytyl *stay at Home!*
Cenacle / And repute not thy self vertuous by heryng
saye, as done men of the courte / But do payne to be
12 verytable by theffecte of the werke / wherto coueytest
thou the gloryes of palayses, whyche for theyr wretched
myserye haue nede that men haue pyte *on them / Ne [* leaf iiij. back]
poursewe it not in fayt / But by the playnt of myn
16 vnhappynes / folowe not me / by cause I am[3] oftymes *Do not follow me*
cladde wyth the beste[4] / But haue pyte and compassion
of the peryls / of whyche I am asseged / and of
thassaultes of whyche I am enuyronned nyght and *who am surrounded with*
20 day / For I haue nede to beholde on what foot that *traitors, and must watch my every word.*
euery man cometh to me / And to note and marke the
paas and the peryl of euery worde that departeth fro
my mouth, to thende that by my vtteraunce I be not
24 surprysed / and that in spekyng vnpourueydly, I ne
gyue mater to ony man to make false relacion / ne to
interprete euyl my worde / whyche I maye neuer
reuoke ne put in agayn / For the courte is the nourysshe *The Court breeds men who study*
28 of peple / whyche by fraude and franchyse / studye for *to entrap you in talk,*
to drawe from one and other[5] suche wordes / by whyche

---

[1] French, "ce a quoi nous *ingerons*," arrogate, claim falsely, misread *jugerons*.—P. M.

[2] French, *souffrance*, patience, endurance.—P. M.

[3] Abridged or translated from a corrupt text. French, "mais par la plainte de mon malheur te chastie (viz. change thy mind), ne ne regarde ou ayes consideration a ce que je suis . . ."—P. M.

[4] Rather, "with the beste-cladde"; French, "avec les mieux vestuz."—P. M.

[5] "Les uns des autres," the one from the other.—P. M.

that they may, by disclosing it, curry favour of the great.

You are soon supplanted by a new-comer,

or, if you keep your Place,

envious men

will give bribes to get it from you; and then you must bribe too.

But in private life, in your own house, you are free.

[* leaf v.]

they may persecute them / by that / whyche by the perylles[1] of other / they may entre in to the grace of them that haue auctoryte to helpe / or to annoye / And whyche take more playsyr in false reportes / than in verytable and trewe wordes / yf thou haue offyce in courte / make the redy to fyghte / For yf thou haue ony good / other shal desyre to take it fro the / and thou shalt not escape wythout debate / Somme shal machyne by somme moyen to deceyue the / And the behoueth to tormente thy self to resist hym / And after whan thou shalt haue employed thy body / thy tyme and thy goodes for to deffende the / Another newe one cometh to the courte, & shal supplante thy benediction / And shal take it gylefully fro the / Thus shalt thou lese wyth grete sorowe / that whyche thou haste goten wyth grete labour / Or yf thyn offyce abyde wyth the / so shal thou not abyde longe wythout drede and fere of hym, or of other enuyous whyche shal laboure to take it fro the / Tofore that thou hast ony offyces Thou boughtest peas and moderacion to lyue / And as sone as thou shalt haue it / thou shalt be deffyed of an other / which shal enforce hym for to gyue largely for to take i fro the ; And the behoueth, maulgre thy self / that thou gyue as moche as he / to thende that thou kepe it / And that it abyde wyth the /

Beholde thenne, brother, beholde / how moche thy lytyl hous gyueth the liberte and franchyse / And thanke it that it hath receyuyd the as only lorde / And after that thy dore is shette and closed, ther entreth none other but suche as pleseth the / Men knocke oftymes atte yates of ryche and hye palayses / Ther is alleway *noyse and murmure / In grete places ben grete and moche peples / of whyche somme ben harde pressyd / The halle of a grete prynce is comunely

4

8

12

16

20

24

28

32

---

[1] French, "ad ce que, au moyen des parolles d'autruy qu'ils rapportent."—P. M.

Infecte and eschaufed of the breeth of the peple / The vssher smyteth wyth hys Rodde vpon the heedes of them that ben there / Somme entre by forse of threst-
4 yng / And other stryue for to resyste / Somme tyme a poure man meschaunt that hath to-fore be sore sette abacke, is further sette forth than an other / And the most fyers and prowde whom a man durste not tofore
8 touche / is put further aback, and is in more gretter daunger / There knoweth noman in certayn yf hys astate be sure or not / But who someuer it be, alway he is in doubte of hys fortune / And whan thou wenest to
12 be most in grace / Thenne remembre the [wordes] of the poete that sayth / that it is no grete preysynge / for to haue ben in the grace of a grete prynce[1] / And to thende that thou mayst the better knowe now the courte / I
16 wyl dyscryue and dyffyne it to the /

The courte, to thende that thou vnderstande it / is a couente of peple that, vnder fayntyse of Comyn wele, assemble hem to gydre for to deceyue eche other / For
20 ther be not many of them but that they selle, bye / or eschange somtyme theyr rentes or propre vestementis / For emonge vs of the courte / we be meschaunt[2] and newfangle / that we bye the other peple / And somm-
24 tyme for theyr money we selle to them our humanyte precyous / we bye other / And other bye vs / But we can moche better selle our self to them that haue to doo wyth vs / how moche thenne mayst thou gete /
28 that it be certayn / or what sewrte / that it be wythout doubte and wythout peryll / wylt thou goo to the court for to selle or lese / the goodnes of vertues whyche thou haste goten wythoute the courte / I saye to the,
32 whan thou enforcest the to entre / thenne begynnest thou to lese the seygnorye of thy self / And thou shalt

A Prince's hall is infected with people's breath. The Usher hits them on the head with his rod.

No one is safe in his situation.

There's no merit in having a Prince's favour.

The Court is an assemblage of mutual deceivers,

who buy and sell one another.

Any one who enters it, loses the rule of himself,

---

[1] Principibus placuisse viris non ultima laus est.—Horat. Epist. I, xvii. 35.—P. M.

[2] Fr. "marchans affaictez," tricky dealers.—P. M.

nomore enioye the droytes and ryghtes of thy franchyse
and liberte / Certes, brother, thou demandest that /
whyche thou oughtest to deffye / And fyxest thyn
hope in that / that shal drawe the to peryl and 4
perdicion / And yf thou come / the courte shal serue
the with so many contryued lesynges on that one
parte / And on that other syde, she shal delyuere to
the so many cures and charges / that thou shalt haue 8
wythin thy self contynuell bataylle / thought / and
anguysshes / And for certayn a man may[1] not *wel
saye / that he is wel happy / that in tyme of tempeste
is bought, and in so many contrarytees assayeed and 12
prouved /

And yf thou demandest / what is the lyf of them
of the courte, I answere the, brother / that it is a poure
rychesse / An habundance myserable / an hyenesse that 16
falleth / An estate not stable / A sewrte tremblyng /
And an euyl lyf[2] / And also it may be called of them
that ben amorouse, a deserte lyberte[3] / Flee, ye men, flee,
and holde and kepe you ferre fro suche an assemblee / 20
yf ye wyll lyue wel and surely / and as peple wel
assured vpon the Ryuage / beholde vs drowne by our
own agreement / And mespryse our blyndenes / that
may ne wylle knowe our propre meschyef / For lyke as 24
the folysshe maronners / whyche somtyme cause them
self to be drowned / by theyr dyspoureyed aduyse-
ment / In lyke wyse the courte draweth to hym and
deceyueth the symple men / and maketh them to desire 28
and coueyte it / lyke as a Rybaulde or a comyn
womman wel arayed / by her lawhyng and by her
kyssynge / The courte taketh meryly them that comen
therto / in vsyng to them false promesses / The courte 32

---

[1] *Orig.* man.
[2] Fr. "ainsi comme un *pillier* tremblant et une moureuse (*al.* mortelle) vie."—P. M.
[3] French, "de ceux qui sont amoureux de sainte liberté." Caxton read *deserte* instead of *de sainte*.—P. M.

The happiness of Private Life, the evils of Court-Life. 15

lawheth atte begynnyng on them that entre / And
after she grymmeth on them / And somtyme byteth *When they come, it bites them.*
them ryght aygrely / The courte reteyneth the caytyuys
4 whiche can not absente and kepe them fro thene / and
alday adnewe[1] auctoryse and lorshippe vpon suche as
they surmounte / The courte also by errour forgeteth *It forgets those who serve it,*
ofte them that beste seruen / And dyspende folyly her *and spend their money on it.*
8 propre good for tenryche them that ben not worthy /
and that haue ryght euyl deseruyd it / And the man is
vnhappy that is taken in / and had leuer to perysshe /
than to yssue and goo out / And ther to lose hys cours
12 of nature / wythout euer to haue hys franchyse and
lyberte vntyl hys´deth / Beleue surely, brother, and *Be sure, Brother,*
doubte nothynge, that thou excersysest ryght good and *that you are doing right in keeping*
ryght prouffytable offyce yf thou canst wel vse thy *to your own house.*
16 maystryse that thou hast in thy lytyl hous / and thou
art and shal be puyssaunt as longe as thou hast, and
shal haue of thy self, suffysaunce / For who that hath
a smal howshold and lytle meyne, and gouerneth them
20 wysely & in peas / he is a lorde / And somoche more is
he ewrous & happy as he more frely maynteneth it /
As ther is nothyng so precious vnder heuen / as for to *Freedom is the most precious thing under heaven.*
be of sufficient comynycacion wyth franchyse[2] /
24 O fortuned men / O blessyd famyllye, where as is
honeste *pouerte that is content with reson, without [* leaf vj.]
etyng the fruytes of other mennes labour / O wel happy
howse, in whyche is vertue wythout fraude ne barat /
28 and whyche is honestly gouerned in the drede of god
and good moderacion of lyf / There entre no synnes /
There is a true and ryghtful lyf / where as is remorse *Private life is rightful,*
of euery synne, and where is no noyse / murmure ne
32 enuye / of suche lyf enioyeth nature / and in smale[3]
eases lyueth she longe / and lytyl and lytyl she cometh *and comes to an honest old age.*

[1] French *advoue*, asserts his authority.—P. M.
[2] Absurd! French, "*commutation contre franchise*," exchangeable value for freedom.—P. M.
[3] French *telles*, such.—P. M.

D

to playsaunt age and honeste ende / For as seyth
Seneke in his tragedyes / Age cometh to late to peple
of smale howses / whyche lyue in suffysaunce / But
emong vs courtyours that be seruauntes to fortune / we 4
lyue disordynatly / we wexen old more by force of
charges than by the nombre of yeres / And by defaulte
of wel lyuyng, we ben wery of the swetenes of our lyf /
whyche so moche we desire, and haste to goo to the 8
deth, the whyche we somoche drede and doubte /
Suffyse the thenne, broder, to lyue in peas on thy
partye / & lerne to contente the by our meschiefs / Ne
mesprise not thy self so moche / that thou take the 12
deth / for the lyf / [1]Ne leue not the goodes that thou
shalt be constrayned to brynge / For to seche to gete
them after wyth grete wayllynges and sorow / whych
shal be to the, horryble and harde to fynde[1] / Fynably 16
I praye the / counseylle and warne the / that yf thou
hast taken[2] ony holy and honeste lyf / that thou wyl
not goo and lese it / And that thou take away that
thought, And despyse[3] alle thy wyl for to come to 20
courte / And be content to wythdrawe the wythin
thenclose of thy pryue hous / And yf thou haue not in
tyme passed knowen that thou hast ben ewrous And
happy / thenne lerne now to knowe it fro hens forth / 24
And to god I comande the by thys wrytyng, whyche
gyue the hys grace / Amen.

Thus endeth the Curial made by maystre Alain
Charretier, Translated thus in Englyssh by Wylliam 28
Caxton.

Courtiers get weary of life; they haste to their death.

If, Brother, you have begun an honourable life, don't lose it by coming to Court!

[1-1] Caxton seems to have misunderstood the French : " Ne delaisse pas a faire le bien que tu serois contraint de reparer par après a grans regrets pour querir ce que te seroit horrible a trouver.—P. M.

[2] French, "se tu prises," if thou appreciatest.—P. M.

[3] French, *disposes* (Du Chesne, *dissipes*), not *despises*.— P. M.

INTRODUCTION TO THE *BALADE*.

By PROF. PAUL MEYER.

Caxton probably found in his manuscript of the French *Curial* the original of the ballad which he printed at the end of his translation. It is not, however, so far as I can ascertain, included in any manuscript or printed collection of Chartier's works. Thanks to my friend E. Picot's unparalleled knowledge of xv[th] century French poetry, I have been able to trace various copies of it. It seems to have been printed first about the end of the xv[th] cent., in the *Jardin de plaisance et fleur de réthorique* (first edition, Paris, Verard, 1499 or 1500).[1] It appears in Olivier Arnoullet's edition (1520—1530) at fol. 73 v°, among some ballads which recent editors have attributed to Villon. From the *Jardin de plaisance*, our ballad was transferred by Jannet to his edition of Villon (Paris, 1867, p. 142). It occurs also, printed from a Brussels MS., in *La danse aux aveugles et autres poésies du xve siécle, extraites de la Bibliothèque des Ducs de Bourgogne* (Lille, A. J. Panckoucke, MDCCXLVIII, 12°), p. 273, and has been recently edited from a Lyon MS., in a provincial periodical, *Lyon-Revue*, 1886, p. 307. The ballad is anonymous in all these texts, and so it is in MS. Bibl. Nat. Fr., 1881, fol. 218 (xv[th] cent.), and 2206, fol. 106 (early xvi[th]). But in the British Museum MS., Lansdowne 380, fol. 220, it is attributed to Alain Chartier.[2] Still the authorship remains doubtful. It has been supposed by Heer Bijvanck, in his *Specimen d'un essai critique sur les œuvres de François Villon* (Leyde, 1882, in 8°), p. 49, that our ballad was the model from which Villon composed his ballad, *Il n'est soing que quant on a fain* (printed by Bijvanck, p. 219, from a Stockholm MS., and presenting Villon's name in acrostic), but it does not follow that the original is Chartier's, the attribution to this author resting only on the authority of the Lansdowne MS., and to a certain extent on Caxton, who seems to have considered it as Chartier's work. One thing is certain, viz. that it is not Villon's, notwithstanding a certain resemblance to his style, as it is by no means likely that the same poet composed two ballads on the same rhymes.

[1] See Brunet, *Manuel du libraire*, JARDIN.
[2] " Ballade faicte et composee par le doulx poete, Maistre Alain Charretier," fo. 218, MS. 380, 8vo.—Catalogue of the Lansdowne MSS., p. 111, col. 2.

Here follows the text of the French ballad from the Paris MS., Bibl. Nat. 1881, with various readings from the *Jardin de plaisance*.[1] The text of MS. 2206 does not differ from that of the Jardin; both omit the same verse in the third stanza. The text of the *Danse aux aveugles* is incorrect, and diverges considerably from the one adopted here, as well as from Caxton.

Il n'est dangie[r] que de villain,
N'orgueul que de povre enrechiz,
Ne [si] sur chemin que le plain,
Ne secours que de vray ami,   4
Ne desespoir que de jalousie,
Ne hault vouloir que d'amoureux,
Ne paistre qu'en grant seignorie,
Ne chiere que d'omme joyeux.   8

Ne servir que de roy souverain,
Ne lait nom que d'omme ahonty,
Ne mangier fors quant on a fain,
N'emprise que d'omme hardi,
Ne povreté que maladie,   12
Ne hante[r] que les bons et preux,
Ne maison que la bien garnie,
Ne chiere que d'omme joieux.   16

Et n'est richasse qu'estre sain,
N'en amours tel bien que mercy,
Ne que la mort riens plus certain,
Ne meilleur chasty que de luy,   20
Ne tel tresor que predommie
N'engoise qu'en cuer couvoiteux
Ne puissance ou il n'ait envie,
Ne chiere que d'omme joyeux.   24

Que voulez vous que je vous die?
Il n'est parler que gracieux,
Ne louer gens qu' après leur vie
Ne chiere que d'omme joyeux.   28

---

[1] Indicated as *J.* in the footnotes.
3 [*si*] from J.   5 The line has its proper length in J., where *de* is left out. 6 J. *N'angoisse que cueur convoiteux* (see l. 22).   7 J. *Ne puissance ou il n'ait envie.*   9 J. *qu' au roy.*   10 MS. *ahontey.*   17 J. *Ne r. que d'estre.* 20 MS. *chastey.*   22 This line is left out in J. (see v. 6).   23 J. *Ne paistre qu'en grant seigneurie.*

[BALADE BY ALAIN CHARTIER.]

(1)

Ther ne is dangyer / but of a vylayn,   [leaf vj. back]
Ne pride / but of a poure man enryched,
Ne so sure a way / as is the playn,   *There is no road so sure as a level one,*
Ne socour / but of a trewe frende,   4
Ne despayr / but of Ialousye,
Ne hye corage / but of one Amorouse,
Ne pestilence[1] / but in grete seygnorye,
    Ne chyere / but of a man Ioyous.   8 *and no cheer but a joyous man's.*

(2)

Ne seruyse / lyke to the kyng souerayn,
Ne fowle name / but of a man shamed,   *There is no foul name, but of a man who is shamed.*
Ne mete / but whan a man hath hungre,
Ne entrepryse / but of a man hardy,   12
Ne pouerte / lyke vnto maladye,
Ne to haunte / but the good and wyse,
Ne howse / but yf it be wel garnysshed,
    Ne chyere / but of a man Ioyous.   16

(3)

Ne ther is no rychesshe / but in helthe,   *There is no riches but in health.*
Ne loue / so good as mercy,
Ne than the deth / nothyng more certayn,
Ne none better chastysed / than of hym self,   20
Ne tresour / lyke vnto wysedom,   *There is no treasure like Wisdom.*
Ne anguysshe / but of ay herte coueytous,
Ne puyssaunce[2] / but ther men haue enuye,
    Ne chyere / but of a man Ioyous.   24

[*Envoy.*]

What wylle ye that I saye?
Ther is no speche / but it be curtoys,
Ne preysyng of men / but after theyr lyf,
    Ne chyer but of a man Ioyous.   28 *There is no cheer but a joyous man's.*

    Caxton

---

[1] Caxton may have read *peste.*—P. M.   [2] *orig.* pnyssaunce

GLOSSARY.

adioustest, 1/25, urgest, bringest forward.
adnewe, 15/5, renew? But see footnote.
appetyteth, 3/5, Fr. *Appeter*. To couet, long for, lust after ... affect, fancie, desire much.
asseged, 11/18, Fr. *Assiegé* . . Besieged, beleaguered.
aualed, 6/1, debased.
auctoryse, *n.* 15/5, authority, oppression. Fr. *vb. Auctoriser, Authoriser.*
aygrely, 15/3, sharply.
barat, 15/27, cheating.
benediction, 12/14, good name and fame; good place, office.
Caduque, 10/1, Fr. *Caduque:* com. Fraile, caduke, feeble, ruinous, readie to fall, vnable to support it selfe.
Cenacle, 11/10, Fr. *Cenacle, Senacle*. A height, or storie in a building.
conne, 4/26, 8/2, know how to, be able, can.
corage, 3/7, heart, spirit, mind.
courrour, 7/25, courier, runer, runner.
courteynes, 5/13, ? courts, or cabinets.
Curyall, or courtly, 4/29.
deffye, 14/3, Fr. *Deffier*. To mistrust.
despoyntement, 5/28, loss of office, fall.
disaccustomme, *vt.* 7/19, put out of custom or habit, change.
domageus, 8/19, hurtful.
droytes, 10/21, 14/1, Fr. *Droict* . . right, law . . equitie . . a mans due ... priuiledge .. power
dyspourveyed, 14/26, unconsiderd, ill-considerd, Fr. *Despourveu*.
empesshe, *vt.* 2/1, Fr. *Empescher*. To . . pester, trouble, disturbe, incomber.
enclose, 16/22, enclosure, walls.
enfayned, 10/20, hypocritical, untrustworthy.
enhaunce, *vt.* 4/30, 5/18, 6/3, 24, advance, exalt; enhaunsyng, 5/26, 7/1.
enioyed, 2/19, glad, rejoiced at.
enpayre, 7/3, Fr. *Empirer*, make worse.
enpesshyng, 4/3, Fr. *Empeschement* . . a let, stop, hinderance, disturbance, comber.
eschaufed, 13/1, heated.
ewrous, 5/15, 15/21, Fr. *Eureux, Heureux* . . Happie, blessed ... prosperous, luckie, fortunate.
exercite, 3/21, Fr. *Exercice* . . vse, practise, action.
fayntyse, 13/18, pretense.
fortuned, 15/24, Fr. *Fortuné* . . Fortunate, happie, luckie; also, made fortunate, blessed with good hap.
fraunchyse, 2/29, 9/15, Fr. *Franchise* . . freenesse, libertie, freedome.
fynably, 16/16, Fr. *Finablement, Finalement*. Finally . . at the last; in summe, in conclusion, in the end.
grymmeth, 6/25, 15/2, looks grim, frowns at.
haunte, 19/14, Fr. *Hanter*. To . . resort vnto; to be familiar with; to conuerse, or commerce with.
indewly, 11/3, unduly.
machyne, *vt.* 12/9, scheme; Fr. *Machiner*. To machinate; frame; contrive, deuise; to practise, plot, conspire against.
meschaunte, *a.* 2/33, 14/23, 13/22, Fr. *Meschant*. Who has no chance, unlucky, miserable.
meschef, 5/25, mishap, ill fortune.
mesprysement, 3/9, undervaluing, disdain.
misprysest, 3/7, Fr. *Mespriser*. To disesteeme, contemne, disdaine, despise, neglect, make light of, set nought by.
mondaynes, 9/21, Fr. *Mondain* . . mundane, worldlie, secular.
nourysshe, 11/27, Fr. *Nourrisse, Nourrice:* f. A Nurse.
ouerseen, 3/13, deceived, mistaken.
ouerthrowe, *vi.* 6/12, tumble over, upset.
poursewe, 3/16, 5/32, Fr. *Poursuyr* (an old word), as *Poursuivre* . . eagerly to follow or chose; earnestly to proceed in, or goe on with.
reffuse, 9/20, Fr. *Refuser*. Refuse.
resteth, 5/19, there remains.
saye, *n.* 11/11, talk, gossip; or *vb.* (hearing men) talk.
surmounte, 15/6, Fr. *Surmonter*. To surmount, surpasse, get before . . to subdue, vanquish, ouercome.
thene, 15/4, thence?
tonne, *n.* 9/18, barrel.
vnpourueydly, 11/24, without forethought, unpremeditatedly, Fr. *Pourveoir, Pourvoir*, to provide.
verbal, or ful of wordes, 10/21.
vermyne, *n.* 9/3, bugs, &c.
wythdraught, *n.* 7/23, withdrawing-room.

Early English Text Society

OFFICERS AND COUNCIL

Honorary Director
PROFESSOR NORMAN DAVIS, M.B.E.
Merton College, Oxford

PROFESSOR J. A. W. BENNETT
PROFESSOR BRUCE DICKINS, F.B.A.
A. I. DOYLE
PROFESSOR P. HODGSON
MISS P. M. KEAN

N. R. KER, F.B.A.
PROFESSOR J. R. R. TOLKIEN
PROFESSOR D. WHITELOCK, F.B.A.
PROFESSOR R. M. WILSON
PROFESSOR C. L. WRENN

Honorary Secretary
R. W. BURCHFIELD
40 Walton Crescent, Oxford

Bankers
THE NATIONAL PROVINCIAL BANK LTD.
Cornmarket Street, Oxford

THE Subscription to the Society, which constitutes full membership, is £3. 3s. (U.S. members $9.00) a year for the annual publications, due in advance on the 1st of JANUARY, and should be paid by Cheque, Postal Order, or Money Order made out to 'The Early English Text Society' and crossed 'National Provincial Bank Limited', to the Hon. Secretary, R. W. Burchfield, 40 Walton Crescent, Oxford. Individual members of the Society are allowed, after consultation with the Secretary, to select other volumes of the Society's publications instead of those for the current year. The Society's Texts can also be purchased separately from the Publisher, Oxford University Press, through a bookseller, at the prices put after them in the List, or through the Secretary, by members only, for their own use, at a discount of 2d. in the shilling.

The Early English Text Society was founded in 1864 by Frederick James Furnivall, with the help of Richard Morris, Walter Skeat, and others, to bring the mass of unprinted Early English literature within the reach of students and provide sound texts from which the New English Dictionary could quote. In 1867 an Extra Series was started of texts already printed but not in satisfactory or readily obtainable editions. At a cost of nearly £35,000, 159 volumes were issued in the Original Series and 126 in the Extra Series before 1921. In that year the title *Extra Series* was dropped, and all the publications of 1921 and subsequent years have since been listed and numbered as part of the

Original Series. Since 1921 more than ninety volumes have been issued. In this prospectus the Original Series and Extra Series for the years 1867-1920 are amalgamated, so as to show all the publications of the Society in a single list. In 1963 the prices of all volumes down to O.S. 222, and still available, were increased by one half, and the prices of some texts after O.S. 222, were also increased, in order to obtain additional revenue for the reprinting of the Society's publications which are at present out of print.

LIST OF PUBLICATIONS
Original Series, 1864-1965. Extra Series, 1867-1920

O.S. 1. **Early English Alliterative Poems**, ed. R. Morris. (*Reprinted* 1965.) 42s.   1864
    2. **Arthur**, ed. F. J. Furnivall. (*Reprinted* 1965.) 7s. 6d.   „
    3. **Lauder on the Dewtie of Kyngis, &c.**, 1556, ed. F. Hall. (*Reprinted* 1965.) 12s. 6d.   „
    4. **Sir Gawayne and the Green Knight**, ed. R. Morris. (*Out of print, see* O.S. 210.)   „
    5. **Hume's Orthographie and Congruitie of the Britan Tongue**, ed. H. B. Wheatley. (*Reprinted* 1965.) 12s. 6d.   1865
    6. **Lancelot of the Laik**, ed. W. W. Skeat. (*Out of print.*)   „
    7. **Genesis & Exodus**, ed. R. Morris. (*Out of print.*)   „
    8. **Morte Arthure**, ed. E. Brock. (*Reprinted* 1961.) 25s.   „
    9. **Thynne on Speght's ed. of Chaucer**, A.D. 1599, ed. G. Kingsley and F. J. Furnivall. (*Out of print.*)   „
   10. **Merlin**, Part I, ed. H. B. Wheatley. (*Out of print.*)
   11. **Lyndesay's Monarche, &c.**, ed. J. Small. Part I. (*Out of print.*)   „
   12. **The Wright's Chaste Wife**, ed. F. J. Furnivall. (*Out of print.*)   „
   13. **Seinte Marherete**, ed. O. Cockayne. (*Out of print, see* O.S. 193.)   1866
   14. **King Horn, Floriz and Blauncheflur, &c.**, ed. J. R. Lumby, re-ed. G. H. McKnight. (*Reprinted* 1962.) 30s.   „
   15. **Political, Religious, and Love Poems**, ed. F. J. Furnivall. (*Out of print.*)   „
   16. **The Book of Quinte Essence**, ed. F. J. Furnivall. (*Out of print.*)   „
   17. **Parallel Extracts from 45 MSS. of Piers the Plowman**, ed. W. W. Skeat. (*Out of print.*)   „
   18. **Hali Meidenhad**, ed. O. Cockayne, re-ed. F. J. Furnivall. (*Out of print.*)   „
   19. **Lyndesay's Monarche, &c.**, ed. J. Small. Part II. (*Out of print.*)   „
   20. **Richard Rolle de Hampole, English Prose Treatises of**, ed. G. G. Perry. (*Reprinted* 1920.) 10s.   „
   21. **Merlin**, ed. H. B. Wheatley. Part II. (*Out of print.*)   „
   22. **Partenay** or **Lusignen**, ed. W. W. Skeat. 10s.   „
   23. **Dan Michel's Ayenbite of Inwyt**, ed. R. Morris and P. Gradon. Vol. I, Text. (*Reissued* 1965.) 50s.   „
   24. **Hymns to the Virgin and Christ; The Parliament of Devils, &c.**, ed. F. J. Furnivall. (*Out of print.*)   1867
   25. **The Stacions of Rome, the Pilgrims' Sea-voyage, with Clene Maydenhod**, ed. F. J. Furnivall. (*Out of print.*)   „
   26. **Religious Pieces in Prose and Verse**, from R. Thornton's MS., ed. G. G. Perry. (*See under* 1913.) (*Out of print.*)   „
   27. **Levins' Manipulus Vocabulorum, a rhyming Dictionary**, ed. H. B. Wheatley. 21s.   „
   28. **William's Vision of Piers the Plowman**, ed. W. W. Skeat. A-Text. (*Reprinted* 1956.) 30s.   „
   29. **Old English Homilies** (1220-30), ed. R. Morris. Series I, Part I. (*Out of print.*)   „
   30. **Pierce the Ploughmans Crede**, ed. W. W. Skeat. (*Out of print.*)   „
E.S. 1. **William of Palerne** or **William and the Werwolf**, re-ed. W. W. Skeat. (*Out of print.*)   „
    2. **Early English Pronunciation**, by A. J. Ellis. Part I. (*Out of print.*)   „
O.S. 31. **Myrc's Duties of a Parish Priest**, in Verse, ed. E. Peacock. (*Out of print.*)   1868
   32. **Early English Meals and Manners: the Boke of Norture of John Russell, the Bokes of Keruynge, Curtasye, and Demeanor, the Babees Book, Urbanitatis, &c.**, ed. F. J. Furnivall. (*Out of print.*)   „
   33. **The Book of the Knight of La Tour-Landry**, ed. T. Wright. (*Out of print.*)   „
   34. **Old English Homilies** (before 1300), ed. R. Morris. Series I, Part II. (*Out of print.*)   „
   35. **Lyndesay's Works**, Part III: The Historie and Testament of Squyer Meldrum, ed. F. Hall. (*Reprinted* 1965.) 12s. 6d.   „
E.S. 3. **Caxton's Book of Curtesye**, in Three Versions, ed. F. J. Furnivall. (*Out of print.*)   „
    4. **Havelok the Dane**, re-ed. W. W. Skeat. (*Out of print.*)   „
    5. **Chaucer's Boethius**, ed. R. Morris. (*Out of print.*)   „
    6. **Chevelere Assigne**, re-ed. Lord Aldenham. (*Out of print.*)   „
O.S. 36. **Merlin**, ed. H. B. Wheatley. Part III. On Arthurian Localities, by J. S. Stuart Glennie. (*Out of print.*)   1869
   37. **Sir David Lyndesay's Works**, Part IV, Ane Satyre of the thrie Estaitis, ed. F. Hall. (*Out of print.*)   „
   38. **William's Vision of Piers the Plowman**, ed. W. W. Skeat. Part II. Text B. (*Reprinted* 1964.) 40s.   „
   39. **The Gest Hystoriale of the Destruction of Troy**, ed. D. Donaldson and G. A. Panton. Part I. (*Out of print.*)   „
E.S. 7. **Early English Pronunciation**, by A. J. Ellis. Part II. (*Out of print.*)   „
    8. **Queene Elizabethes Achademy, &c.**, ed. F. J. Furnivall. Essays on early Italian and German Books of Courtesy, by W. M. Rossetti and E. Oswald. (*Out of print.*)   „

The Original and Extra Series of the 'Early English Text Society'

E.S. 9. Awdeley's Fraternitye of Vacabondes, Harman's Caveat, &c., ed. E. Viles and F. J. Furnivall. (*Out of print.*) 1869
O.S. 40. **English Gilds,** their Statutes and Customs, A.D. 1389, ed. Toulmin Smith and Lucy T. Smith, with an Essay on Gilds and Trades-Unions, by L. Brentano. (*Reprinted* 1963.) 55*s.* 1870
41. William Lauder's Minor Poems, ed. F. J. Furnivall. (*Out of print.*) „
42. Bernardus De Cura Rei Famuliaris, Early Scottish Prophecies, &c., ed. J. R. Lumby. (*Reprinted* 1965.) 12*s.* 6*d.* „
43. Ratis Raving, and other Moral and Religious Pieces, ed. J. R. Lumby. (*Out of print.*) „
E.S. 10. Andrew Boorde's Introduction of Knowledge, 1547, Dyetary of Helth, 1542, Barnes in Defence of the Berde, 1542–3, ed. F. J. Furnivall. (*Out of print.*) „
11. Barbour's Bruce, ed. W. W. Skeat. Part I. 21*s.* „
O.S. 44. The Alliterative Romance of Joseph of Arimathie, or The Holy Grail: from the Vernon MS.; with W. de Worde's and Pynson's Lives of Joseph: ed. W. W. Skeat. (*Out of print.*) 1871
45. King Alfred's West-Saxon Version of Gregory's Pastoral Care, ed., with an English translation, by Henry Sweet. Part I. (*Reprinted* 1958.) 45*s.* „
46. Legends of the Holy Rood, Symbols of the Passion and Cross Poems, ed. R. Morris. (*Out of print.*) „
47. Sir David Lyndesay's Works, ed. J. A. H. Murray. Part V. (*Out of print.*) „
48. The Times' Whistle, and other Poems, by R. O., 1616; ed. J. M. Cowper. (*Out of print.*) „
E.S. 12. **England in Henry VIII's Time:** a Dialogue between Cardinal Pole and Lupset, by Thom. Starkey Chaplain to Henry VIII, ed. J. M. Cowper. Part II. (*Out of print,* Part I is E.S. 32, 1878.) „
13. A Supplicacyon of the Beggers, by Simon Fish, A.D. 1528–9, ed. F. J. Furnivall, with A Supplication to our Moste Soueraigne Lorde, A Supplication of the Poore Commons, and The Decaye of England by the Great Multitude of Sheep, ed. J. M. Cowper. (*Out of print.*) „
14. Early English Pronunciation, by A. J. Ellis. Part III. (*Out of print.*) „
O.S. 49. An Old English Miscellany, containing a Bestiary, Kentish Sermons, Proverbs of Alfred, and Religious Poems of the 13th cent., ed. R. Morris. (*Out of print.*) 1872
50. King Alfred's West-Saxon Version of Gregory's Pastoral Care, ed. H. Sweet. Part II. (*Reprinted* 1958) 45*s.* „
51. Þe Liflade of St. Juliana, 2 versions, with translations; ed. O. Cockayne and E. Brock. (*Reprinted* 1957.) 37*s.* 6*d.* „
52. Palladius on Husbondrie, englisht, ed. Barton Lodge. Part I. (*Out of print.*) „
E.S. 15. Robert Crowley's Thirty-One Epigrams, Voyce of the Last Trumpet, Way to Wealth, &c., ed. J. M. Cowper. (*Out of print.*) „
16. Chaucer's Treatise on the Astrolabe, ed. W. W. Skeat. (*Out of print.*) „
17. The Complaynt of Scotlande, with 4 Tracts, ed. J. A. H. Murray. Part I. (*Out of print.*) „
O.S. 53. Old-English Homilies, Series II, and three Hymns to the Virgin and God, 13th-century, with the music to two of them, in old and modern notation, ed. R. Morris. (*Out of print.*) 1873
54. The Vision of Piers Plowman, ed. W. W. Skeat. Part III. Text C. (*Reprinted* 1959.) 52*s.* 6*d.* „
55. Generydes, a Romance, ed. W. Aldis Wright. Part I. 5*s.* „
E.S. 18. The Complaynt of Scotlande, ed. J. A. H. Murray. Part II. (*Out of print.*) „
19. The Myroure of oure Ladye, ed. J. H. Blunt. (*Out of print.*) „
O.S. 56. The Gest Hystoriale of the Destruction of Troy, in alliterative verse, ed. D. Donaldson and G. A. Panton. Part II. (*Out of print.*) 1874
57. Cursor Mundi, in four Texts, ed. R. Morris. Part I, with 2 photolithographic facsimiles. (*Reprinted* 1961.) 25*s.* „
58. The Blickling Homilies, ed. R. Morris. Part I. (*Out of print.*) „
E.S. 20. Lovelich's History of the Holy Grail, ed. F. J. Furnivall. Part I. (*Out of print.*) „
21. Barbour's Bruce, ed. W. W. Skeat. Part II. (*Out of print.*) „
22. Henry Brinklow's Complaynt of Roderyck Mors and The Lamentacyon of a Christen Agaynst the Cytye of London, made by Roderigo Mors, ed. J. M. Cowper. (*Out of print.*) „
23. Early English Pronunciation, by A. J. Ellis. Part IV. (*Out of print.*) „
O.S. 59. Cursor Mundi, in four Texts, ed. R. Morris. Part II. (*Out of print.*) 1875
60. Meditacyuns on the Soper of our Lorde, by Robert of Brunne, ed. J. M. Cowper. (*Out of print.*) „
61. The Romance and Prophecies of Thomas of Erceldoune, ed. J. A. H. Murray. (*Out of print.*) „
E.S. 24. Lovelich's History of the Holy Grail, ed. F. J. Furnivall. Part II. (*Out of print.*) „
25. Guy of Warwick, 15th-century Version, ed. J. Zupitza. Part I. (*Out of print.*) „
O.S. 62. Cursor Mundi, in four Texts, ed. R. Morris. Part III. (*Out of print.*) 1876
63. The Blickling Homilies, ed. R. Morris. Part II. (*Out of print.*) „
64. Francis Thynne's Embleames and Epigrams, ed. F. J. Furnivall. 12*s.* 6*d.* „
65. Be Domes Dæge (Bede's *De Die Judicii*), &c., ed. J. R. Lumby. (*Reprinted* 1964.) 30*s.* „
E.S. 26. Guy of Warwick, 15th-century Version, ed. J. Zupitza. Part II. (*Out of print.*) „
27. The English Works of John Fisher, ed. J. E. B. Mayor. Part I. (*Out of print.*) „
O.S. 66. Cursor Mundi, in four Texts, ed. R. Morris. Part IV, with 2 autotypes. (*Out of print.*) 1877
67. Notes on Piers Plowman, by W. W. Skeat. Part I. (*Out of print.*) „
E.S. 28. Lovelich's Holy Grail, ed. F. J. Furnivall. Part III. (*Out of print.*) „
29. Barbour's Bruce, ed. W. W. Skeat. Part III. (*Out of print.*) „
O.S. 68. Cursor Mundi, in 4 Texts, ed. R. Morris. Part V. (*Out of print.*) 1878
69. Adam Davie's 5 Dreams about Edward II, &c., ed. F. J. Furnivall. 9*s.* „
70. Generydes, a Romance, ed. W. Aldis Wright. Part II. 7*s.* 6*d.* „
E.S. 30. Lovelich's Holy Grail, ed. F. J. Furnivall. Part IV. (*Out of print.*) „

The Original and Extra Series of the 'Early English Text Society'

E.S. 31.	The Alliterative Romance of Alexander and Dindimus, ed. W. W. Skeat. (*Out of print.*)	1878
32.	Starkey's England in Henry VIII's Time. Part I. **Starkey's Life and Letters**, ed. S. J. Herrtage. 14s.	,,
O.S. 71.	The Lay Folks Mass-Book, four texts, ed. T. F. Simmons. (*Out of print.*)	1879
72.	Palladius on Husbondrie, englisht, ed. S. J. Herrtage. Part II. 9s.	,,
E.S. 33.	Gesta Romanorum, ed. S. J. Herrtage. (*Reprinted* 1962.) 55s.	,,
34.	The Charlemagne Romances: 1. Sir Ferumbras, from Ashm. MS. 33, ed. S. J. Herrtage. (*Out of print.*)	,,
O.S. 73.	The Blickling Homilies, ed. R. Morris. Part III. (*Out of print.*)	1880
74.	English Works of Wyclif, hitherto unprinted, ed. F. D. Matthew. (*Out of print.*)	,,
E.S. 35.	Charlemagne Romances: 2. The Sege off Melayne, Sir Otuell, &c., ed. S. J. Herrtage. (*Out of print.*)	,,
36.	Charlemagne Romances: 3. Lyf of Charles the Grete, ed. S. J. Herrtage. Part I. (*Out of print.*)	,,
O.S. 75.	Catholicon Anglicum, an English-Latin Wordbook, from Lord Monson's MS., A.D. 1483, ed., with Introduction and Notes, by S. J. Herrtage and Preface by H. B. Wheatley. (*Out of print.*)	1881
76.	Ælfric's Metrical Lives of Saints, in MS. Cott. Jul. E VII, ed. W. W. Skeat. Part I. (*Out of print.*)	,,
E.S. 37.	Charlemagne Romances: 4. Lyf of Charles the Grete, ed. S. J. Herrtage. Part II (*Out of print.*)	,,
38.	Charlemagne Romances: 5. The Sowdone of Babylone, ed. E. Hausknecht. (*Out of print.*)	,,
O.S. 77.	Beowulf, the unique MS. autotyped and transliterated, ed. J. Zupitza. (*Re-issued as* No. 245. *See under* 1958.)	1882
78.	The Fifty Earliest English Wills, in the Court of Probate, 1387–1439, ed. F. J. Furnivall. (*Reprinted* 1964.) 42s.	,,
E.S. 39.	Charlemagne Romances: 6. Rauf Coilyear, Roland, Otuel, &c., ed. S. J. Herrtage. (*Out of print.*)	,,
40.	Charlemagne Romances: 7. Huon of Burdeux, by Lord Berners, ed. S. L. Lee. Part I. (*Out of print.*)	,,
O.S. 79.	King Alfred's Orosius, from Lord Tollemache's 9th-century MS., ed. H. Sweet. Part I. (*Reprinted* 1959.) 45s.	1883
79 b.	Extra Volume. Facsimile of the Epinal Glossary, ed. H. Sweet. (*Out of print.*)	,,
E.S. 41.	Charlemagne Romances: 8. Huon of Burdeux, by Lord Berners, ed. S. L. Lee. Part II. (*Out of print.*)	,,
42.	Guy of Warwick: 2 texts (Auchinleck MS. and Caius MS.), ed. J. Zupitza. Part I. (*Out of print.*)	,,
O.S. 80.	The Life of St. Katherine, B.M. Royal MS. 17 A. xxvii, &c., and its Latin Original, ed. E. Einenkel. (*Out of print.*)	1884
81.	Piers Plowman: Glossary, &c., ed. W. W. Skeat. Part IV, completing the work. (*Out of print.*)	,,
E.S. 43.	Charlemagne Romances: 9. Huon of Burdeux, by Lord Berners, ed. S. L. Lee. Part III. (*Out of print.*)	,,
44.	Charlemagne Romances: 10. The Foure Sonnes of Aymon, ed. Octavia Richardson. Part I. (*Out of print.*)	,,
O.S. 82.	Ælfric's Metrical Lives of Saints, MS. Cott. Jul. E VII, ed. W. W. Skeat. Part II. (*Out of print.*)	1885
83.	The Oldest English Texts, Charters, &c., ed. H. Sweet. (*Reprinted* 1957.) 63s.	,,
E.S. 45.	Charlemagne Romances: 11. The Foure Sonnes of Aymon, ed. O. Richardson. Part II. (*Out of print.*)	,,
46.	Sir Beves of Hamtoun, ed. E. Kölbing. Part I. (*Out of print.*)	,,
O.S. 84.	Additional Analogs to 'The Wright's Chaste Wife', O.S. 12, by W. A. Clouston. 1s. 6d.	1886
85.	The Three Kings of Cologne, ed. C. Horstmann. 30s.	,,
86.	Prose Lives of Women Saints, ed. C. Horstmann. 21s.	,,
E.S. 47.	The Wars of Alexander, ed. W. W. Skeat. (*Out of print.*)	,,
48.	Sir Beves of Hamtoun, ed. E. Kölbing. Part II. (*Out of print.*)	,,
O.S. 87.	The Early South-English Legendary, Laud MS. 108, ed. C. Horstmann. (*Out of print.*)	1887
88.	Hy. Bradshaw's Life of St. Werburghe (Pynson, 1521), ed. C. Horstmann. 18s.	,,
E.S. 49.	Guy of Warwick, 2 texts (Auchinleck and Caius MSS.), ed. J. Zupitza. Part II. (*Out of print.*)	,,
50.	Charlemagne Romances: 12. Huon of Burdeux, by Lord Berners, ed. S. L. Lee. Part IV. (*Out of print.*)	,,
51.	Torrent of Portyngale, ed. E. Adam. (*Out of print.*)	,,
O.S. 89.	Vices and Virtues, ed. F. Holthausen. Part I. (*Out of print.*)	1888
90.	Anglo-Saxon and Latin Rule of St. Benet, interlinear Glosses, ed. H. Logeman. (*Out of print.*)	,,
91.	Two Fifteenth-Century Cookery-Books, ed. T. Austin. (*Reprinted* 1964.) 42s.	,,
E.S. 52.	Bullein's Dialogue against the Feuer Pestilence, 1578, ed. M. and A. H. Bullen. (*Out of print.*)	,,
53.	Vicary's Anatomie of the Body of Man, 1548, ed. 1577, ed. F. J. and Percy Furnivall. Part I. (*Out of print.*)	,,
54.	The Curial made by maystere Alain Charretier, translated by William Caxton, 1484, ed. F. J. Furnivall and P. Meyer. (*Reprinted* 1965.) 10s.	,,
O.S. 92.	Eadwine's Canterbury Psalter, from the Trin. Cambr. MS., ed. F. Harsley, Part II. (*Out of print.*)	1889
93.	Defensor's Liber Scintillarum, ed. E. Rhodes. 30s.	,,
E.S. 55.	Barbour's Bruce, ed. W.W. Skeat. Part IV. (*Out of print.*)	,,
56.	Early English Pronunciation, by A. J. Ellis. Part V, the present English Dialects. (*Out of print.*)	,,
O.S. 94.	Ælfric's Metrical Lives of Saints, MS. Cott. Jul. E VII, ed. W. W. Skeat. Part III. 45s.	1890
95.	The Old-English Version of Bede's Ecclesiastical History, re-ed. T. Miller. Part I, 1. (*Reprinted* 1959.) 45s.	,,
E.S. 57.	Caxton's Eneydos, ed. W. T. Culley and F. J. Furnivall. (*Reprinted* 1962.) 30s.	,,
58.	Caxton's Blanchardyn and Eglantine, c. 1489, ed. L. Kellner. (*Reprinted* 1962.) 42s.	,,
O.S. 96.	The Old-English Version of Bede's Ecclesiastical History, re-ed. T. Miller. Part I, 2. (*Reprinted* 1959.) 45s.	1891
97.	The Earliest English Prose Psalter, ed. K. D. Buelbring. Part I. (*Out of print.*)	,,
E.S. 59.	Guy of Warwick, 2 texts (Auchinleck and Caius MSS.), ed. J. Zupitza. Part III. (*Out of print.*)	,,
60.	Lydgate's Temple of Glas, re-ed. J. Schick. (*Out of print.*)	,,
O.S. 98.	Minor Poems of the Vernon MS., ed. C. Horstmann. Part I. (*Out of print.*)	1892
99.	Cursor Mundi. Preface, Notes, and Glossary, Part VI, ed. R. Morris. (*Reprinted* 1962.) 25s.	,,
E.S. 61.	Hoccleve's Minor Poems, I, from the Phillipps and Durham MSS., ed. F. J. Furnivall. (*Out of print.*)	,,

The Original and Extra Series of the 'Early English Text Society'

E.S. 62. **The Chester Plays**, re-ed. H. Deimling. Part I. (*Reprinted* 1959.) 37s. 6d.   1892
O.S. 100. **Capgrave's Life of St. Katharine**, ed. C. Horstmann, with Forewords by F. J. Furnivall. (*Out of print.*)   1893
     101. **Cursor Mundi**. Essay on the MSS., their Dialects, &c., by H. Hupe. Part VII. (*Reprinted* 1962.) 25s.   ,,
E.S. 63. **Thomas à Kempis's De Imitatione Christi**, ed. J. K. Ingram. (*Out of print.*)   ,,
     64. **Caxton's Godeffroy of Boloyne, or The Siege and Conqueste of Jerusalem**, 1481, ed. Mary N. Colvin. (*Out of print.*)   ,,
O.S. 102. **Lanfranc's Science of Cirurgie**, ed. R. von Fleischhacker. Part I. 36s.   1894
     103. **The Legend of the Cross**, &c., ed. A. S. Napier. (*Out of print.*)   ,,
E.S. 65. **Sir Beves of Hamtoun**, ed. E. Kölbing. Part III. (*Out of print.*)   ,,
     66. **Lydgate's and Burgh's Secrees of Philisoffres** ('Governance of Kings and Princes'), ed. R. Steele. (*Out of print.*)   ,,
O.S. 104. **The Exeter Book** (Anglo-Saxon Poems), re-ed. I Gollancz. Part I. (*Reprinted* 1958.) 45s.   1895
     105. **The Prymer or Lay Folks' Prayer Book**, Camb. Univ. MS., ed. H. Littlehales. Part I. (*Out of print.*) ,,
E.S. 67. **The Three Kings' Sons**, a Romance, ed. F. J. Furnivall. Part I, the Text. (*Out of print.*)   ,,
     68. **Melusine**, the prose Romance, ed. A. K. Donald. Part I, the Text. (*Out of print.*)   ,,
O.S. 106. **R. Misyn's Fire of Love and Mending of Life** (Hampole), ed. R. Harvey. (*Out of print.*)   1896
     107. **The English Conquest of Ireland**, A.D. 1166–1185, 2 Texts, ed. F. J. Furnivall. Part I. 27s.   ,,
E.S. 69. **Lydgate's Assembly of the Gods**, ed. O. L. Triggs. (*Reprinted* 1957.) 37s. 6d.   ,,
     70. **The Digby Plays**, ed. F. J. Furnivall. (*Out of print.*)   ,,
O.S. 108. **Child-Marriages and -Divorces, Trothplights, &c.** Chester Depositions, 1561–6, ed. F. J. Furnivall. (*Out of print.*)   1897
     109. **The Prymer or Lay Folks' Prayer Book**, ed. H. Littlehales. Part II. (*Out of print*)   ,,
E.S. 71. **The Towneley Plays**, ed. G. England and A. W. Pollard. (*Re-issued* 1952.) 45s.   ,,
     72. **Hoccleve's Regement of Princes, and 14 Poems**, ed. F. J. Furnivall. (*Out of print.*)   ,,
     73. **Hoccleve's Minor Poems**, II, from the Ashburnham MS., ed. I. Gollancz. (*Out of print.*)   ,,
O.S. 110. **The Old-English Version of Bede's Ecclesiastical History**, ed. T. Miller. Part II, 1. (*Reprinted* 1963.) 30s.   1898
     111. **The Old-English Version of Bede's Ecclesiastical History**, ed. T. Miller. Part II, 2. (*Reprinted* 1963.) 30s.   ,,
E.S. 74. **Secreta Secretorum**, 3 prose Englishings, one by Jas. Yonge, 1428, ed. R. Steele. Part I. 36s.   ,,
     75. **Speculum Guidonis de Warwyk**, ed. G. L. Morrill. 18s.   ,,
O.S. 112. **Merlin**. Part IV. Outlines of the Legend of Merlin, by W. E. Mead. (*Out of print.*)   1899
     113. **Queen Elizabeth's Englishings of Boethius, Plutarch**, &c., ed. C. Pemberton. (*Out of print.*)   ,,
E.S. 76. **George Ashby's Poems**, &c., ed. Mary Bateson. (*Reprinted* 1965.) 30s.   ,,
     77. **Lydgate's DeGuilleville's Pilgrimage of the Life of Man**, ed. F. J. Furnivall. Part I. (*Out of print.*) ,,
     78. **The Life and Death of Mary Magdalene**, by T. Robinson, c. 1620, ed. H. O. Sommer. 9s.   ,,
O.S. 114. **Ælfric's Metrical Lives of Saints**, ed. W. W. Skeat. Part IV and last. (*Out of print.*)   1900
     115. **Jacob's Well**, ed. A. Brandeis. Part I. 18s.   ,,
     116. **An Old-English Martyrology**, re-ed. G. Herzfeld. (*Out of print.*)   ,,
E.S. 79. **Caxton's Dialogues, English and French**, ed. H. Bradley. 18s.   ,,
     80. **Lydgate's Two Nightingale Poems**, ed. O. Glauning. 9s.   ,,
     80A. **Selections from Barbour's Bruce** (Books I–X), ed. W. W. Skeat. 20s.   ,,
     81. **The English Works of John Gower**, ed. G. C. Macaulay. Part I. (*Reprinted* 1957.) 60s.   ,,
O.S. 117. **Minor Poems of the Vernon MS.**, ed. F. J. Furnivall. Part II. 27s.   1901
     118. **The Lay Folks' Catechism**, ed. T. F. Simmons and H. E. Nolloth. (*Out of print.*)   ,,
     119. **Robert of Brunne's Handlyng Synne**, and its French original, re-ed. F. J. Furnivall. Part I. (*Out of print.*)   ,,
E.S. 82. **The English Works of John Gower**, ed. G. C. Macaulay. Part II. (*Reprinted* 1957.) 60s.   ,,
     83. **Lydgate's DeGuilleville's Pilgrimage of the Life of Man**, ed. F. J. Furnivall. Part II. (*Out of print.*) ,,
     84. **Lydgate's Reason and Sensuality**, ed. E. Sieper. Vol. I. (*Reprinted* 1965.) 42s.   ,,
O.S. 120. **The Rule of St. Benet** in Northern Prose and Verse, and Caxton's Summary, ed. E. A. Kock. (*Out of print.*)   1902
     121. **The Laud MS. Troy-Book**, ed. J. E. Wülfing. Part I. 27s.   ,,
E.S. 85. **Alexander Scott's Poems**, 1568, ed. A. K. Donald. (*Out of print.*)   ,,
     86. **William of Shoreham's Poems**, re-ed. M. Konrath. Part I. (*Out of print.*)   ,,
     87. **Two Coventry Corpus Christi Plays**, re-ed. H. Craig. (*See under* 1952.)   ,,
O.S. 122. **The Laud MS. Troy-Book**, ed. by J. E. Wülfing. Part II. 36s.   1903
     123. **Robert of Brunne's Handlyng Synne**, and its French original, re-ed. F. J. Furnivall. Part II. (*Out of print.*)   ,,
E.S. 88. **Le Morte Arthur**, re-ed. J. D. Bruce. (*Reprinted* 1959.) 45s.   ,,
     89. **Lydgate's Reason and Sensuality**, ed. E. Sieper. Vol. II. (*Reprinted* 1965.) 35s.   ,,
     90. **English Fragments from Latin Medieval Service-Books**, ed. H. Littlehales. (*Out of print.*)   ,,
O.S. 124. **Twenty-six Political and Other Poems** from Digby MS. 102, &c., ed. J. Kail. Part I. 18s.   1904
     125. **Medieval Records of a London City Church**, ed. H. Littlehales. Part I. (*Out of print.*)   ,,
     126. **An Alphabet of Tales**, in Northern English, from the Latin, ed. M. M. Banks. Part I. 18s.   ,,
E.S. 91. **The Macro Plays**, ed. F. J. Furnivall and A. W. Pollard. (*Out of print.*)   ,,
     92. **Lydgate's DeGuilleville's Pilgrimage of the Life of Man**, ed. Katherine B. Locock. Part III. (*Out of print.*) ,,
     93. **Lovelich's Romance of Merlin**, from the unique MS., ed. E. A. Kock. Part I. (*Out of print.*)   ,,
O.S. 127. **An Alphabet of Tales**, in Northern English, from the Latin, ed. M. M. Banks. Part II. 18s.   1905
     128. **Medieval Records of a London City Church**, ed. H. Littlehales. Part II. 18s.   ,,
O.S. 129. **The English Register of Godstow Nunnery**, ed. A. Clark. Part I. 18s.   ,,
E.S. 94. **Respublica**, a Play on a Social England, ed. L. A. Magnus. (*Out of print. See under* 1946.)   ,,

The Original and Extra Series of the 'Early English Text Society'

E.S.	95. Lovelich's History of the Holy Grail. Part V. The Legend of the Holy Grail, ed. Dorothy Kempe. (*Out of print.*)	1905
	96. Mirk's Festial, ed. T. Erbe. Part I. 21s.	,,
O.S.	130. The English Register of Godstow Nunnery, ed. A. Clark. Part II. 27s.	1906
	131. The Brut, or The Chronicle of England, ed. F. Brie. Part I. (*Reprinted* 1960.) 25s.	,,
	132. John Metham's Works, ed. H. Craig. 27s.	,,
E.S.	97. Lydgate's Troy Book, ed. H. Bergen. Part I, Books I and II. (*Out of print.*)	,,
	98. Skelton's Magnyfycence, ed. R. L. Ramsay. (*Reprinted* 1958.) 45s.	,,
	99. The Romance of Emaré, re-ed. Edith Rickert. (*Reprinted* 1958.) 22s. 6d.	,,
O.S.	133. The English Register of Oseney Abbey, by Oxford, ed. A. Clark. Part I. 27s.	1907
	134. The Coventry Leet Book, ed. M. Dormer Harris. Part I. (*Out of print.*)	,,
E.S.	100. The Harrowing of Hell, and The Gospel of Nicodemus, re-ed. W. H. Hulme. (*Reprinted* 1961.) 30s.	,,
	101. Songs, Carols, &c., from Richard Hill's Balliol MS., ed. R. Dyboski. (*Out of print.*)	,,
O.S.	135. The Coventry Leet Book, ed. M. Dormer Harris. Part II. 27s.	1908
	135 b. *Extra Issue.* Prof. Manly's Piers Plowman and its Sequence, urging the fivefold authorship of the Vision. (*Out of print.*)	,,
	136. The Brut, or The Chronicle of England, ed. F. Brie. Part II. (*Out of print.*)	,,
E.S.	102. Promptorium Parvulorum, the 1st English-Latin Dictionary, ed. A. L. Mayhew. 37s. 6d.	,,
	103. Lydgate's Troy Book, ed. H. Bergen. Part II, Book III. (*Out of print.*)	,,
O.S.	137. Twelfth-Century Homilies in MS. Bodley 343, ed. A. O. Belfour. Part I, the Text. (*Reprinted* 1962.) 25s.	1909
	138. The Coventry Leet Book, ed. M. Dormer Harris. Part III. 27s.	,,
E.S.	104. The Non-Cycle Mystery Plays, re-ed. O. Waterhouse. (*Out of print.*)	,,
	105. The Tale of Beryn, with the Pardoner and Tapster, ed. F. J. Furnivall and W. G. Stone. (*Out of print.*)	,,
O.S.	139. John Arderne's Treatises on Fistula in Ano, &c., ed. D'Arcy Power. 27s.	1910
	139 b, c, d, e, f, Extra Issue. The Piers Plowman Controversy: b. Dr. Jusserand's 1st Reply to Prof. Manly; c. Prof. Manly's Answer to Dr. Jusserand; d. Dr. Jusserand's 2nd Reply to Prof. Manly; e. Mr. R. W. Chambers's Article; f. Dr. Henry Bradley's Rejoinder to Mr. R. W. Chambers. (*Out of print.*)	,,
	140. Capgrave's Lives of St. Augustine and St. Gilbert of Sempringham, ed. J. Munro. (*Out of print.*)	,,
E.S.	106. Lydgate's Troy Book, ed. H. Bergen. Part III. (*Out of print.*)	,,
	107. Lydgate's Minor Poems, ed. H. N. MacCracken. Part I. Religious Poems. (*Reprinted* 1961.) 40s.	,,
O.S.	141. Erthe upon Erthe, all the known texts, ed. Hilda Murray. (*Reprinted* 1964.) 30s.	1911
	142. The English Register of Godstow Nunnery, ed. A. Clark. Part III. 18s.	,,
	143. The Prose Life of Alexander, Thornton MS., ed. J. S. Westlake. 18s.	,,
E.S.	108. Lydgate's Siege of Thebes, re-ed. A. Erdmann. Part I, the Text. (*Reprinted* 1960.) 24s.	,,
	109. Partonope, re-ed. A. T. Bödtker. The Texts. (*Out of print.*)	,,
O.S.	144. The English Register of Oseney Abbey, by Oxford, ed. A. Clark. Part II. 18s.	1912
	145. The Northern Passion, ed. F. A. Foster. Part I, the four parallel texts. 27s.	,,
E.S.	110. Caxton's Mirrour of the World, with all the woodcuts, ed. O. H. Prior. (*Out of print.*)	,,
	111. Caxton's History of Jason, the Text, Part I, ed. J. Munro. 27s.	,,
O.S.	146. The Coventry Leet Book, ed. M. Dormer Harris. Introduction, Indexes, &c. Part IV. 18s.	1913
	147. The Northern Passion, ed. F. A. Foster, Introduction, French Text, Variants and Fragments, Glossary. Part II. 27s.	,,
	[An enlarged reprint of O.S. 26, Religious Pieces in Prose and Verse, from the Thornton MS., ed. G. G. Perry. (*Out of print.*)]	,,
E.S.	112. Lovelich's Romance of Merlin, ed. E. A. Kock. Part II. (*Reprinted* 1961.) 30s.	,,
	113. Poems by Sir John Salusbury, Robert Chester, and others, from Christ Church MS. 184, &c., ed. Carleton Brown. 27s.	,,
O.S.	148. A Fifteenth-Century Courtesy Book and Two Franciscan Rules, ed. R. W. Chambers and W. W. Seton. (*Reprinted* 1963.) 25s.	1914
	149 Lincoln Diocese Documents, 1450–1544, ed. Andrew Clark. 27s.	,,
	150. The Old-English Rule of Bp. Chrodegang, and the Capitula of Bp. Theodulf, ed. A. S. Napier. 22s. 6d.	,,
E.S.	114. The Gild of St. Mary, Lichfield, ed. F. J. Furnivall. 27s.	,,
	115. The Chester Plays, re-ed. J. Matthews. Part II. (*Reprinted* 1959.) 37s. 6d.	,,
O.S.	151. The Lanterne of Light, ed. Lilian M. Swinburn. (*Out of print.*)	1915
	152. Early English Homilies, from Cott. Vesp. D. xiv, ed. Rubie Warner. Part I, Text. (*Out of print.*)	,,
E.S.	116. The Pauline Epistles, ed. M. J. Powell. (*Out of print.*)	,,
	117. Bp. Fisher's English Works, ed. R. Bayne. Part II. 27s.	,,
O.S.	153. Mandeville's Travels, ed. P. Hamelius. Part I, Text. (*Reprinted* 1960.) 25s.	1916
	154. Mandeville's Travels, ed. P. Hamelius. Part II, Notes and Introduction. (*Reprinted* 1961.) 25s.	,,
E.S.	118. The Earliest Arithmetics in English, ed. R. Steele. 27s.	,,
	119. The Owl and Nightingale, 2 Texts parallel, ed. G. F. H. Sykes and J. H. G. Grattan. (*Out of print.*)	,,
O.S.	155. The Wheatley MS., ed. Mabel Day. 54s.	1917
E.S.	120. Ludus Coventriae, ed. K. S. Block. (*Reprinted* 1961.) 30s.	,,
O.S.	156. Reginald Pecock's Donet, from Bodl. MS. 916, ed. Elsie V. Hitchcock. 63s.	1918
E.S.	121. Lydgate's Fall of Princes, ed. H. Bergen. Part I. (*Out of print.*)	,,
	122. Lydgate's Fall of Princes, ed. H. Bergen. Part II. (*Out of print.*)	,,
O.S.	157. Harmony of the Life of Christ, from MS. Pepys 2498, ed. Margery Goates. (*Out of print.*)	1919
	158. Meditations on the Life and Passion of Christ, from MS. Add., 11307, ed. Charlotte D'Evelyn. (*Out of print.*)	,,

The Original and Extra Series of the 'Early English Text Society'

E.S. 123. Lydgate's Fall of Princes, ed. H. Bergen. Part III. (*Out of print.*)   1919
124. Lydgate's Fall of Princes, ed. H. Bergen. Part IV. (*Out of print.*)   ,,
O.S. 159 Vices and Virtues, ed. F. Holthausen. Part II. 21*s*.   1920
[A re-edition of O.S. 18, Hali Meidenhad, ed. O. Cockayne, with a variant MS., Bodl. 34, hitherto unprinted, ed. F. J. Furnivall. (*Out of print.*)]
E.S. 125. Lydgate's Siege of Thebes, ed. A. Erdmann and E. Ekwall. Part II. (*Out of print.*)   ,,
126. Lydgate's Troy Book, ed. H. Bergen. Part IV. (*Out of print.*)   ,,

O.S. 160. The Old English Heptateuch, MS. Cott. Claud. B. IV, ed. S. J. Crawford. (*Out of print.*)   1921
161. Three O.E. Prose Texts, MS. Cott. Vit. A. xv, ed. S. Rypins. (*Out of print.*)   ,,
162. Facsimile of MS. Cotton Nero A. x (Pearl, Cleanness, Patience and Sir Gawain), Introduction by I. Gollancz. (*Reprinted* 1955.) 150*s*.   1922
163. Book of the Foundation of St. Bartholomew's Church in London, ed. N. Moore. (*Out of print.*)   1923
164. Pecock's Folewer to the Donet, ed. Elsie V. Hitchcock. (*Out of print.*)   ,,
165. Middleton's Chinon of England, with Leland's Assertio Arturii and Robinson's translation, ed. W. E. Mead. (*Out of print.*)   ,,
166. Stanzaic Life of Christ, ed. Frances A. Foster. (*Out of print.*)   1924
167. Trevisa's Dialogus inter Militem et Clericum, Sermon by FitzRalph, and Bygynnyng of the World, ed. A. J. Perry. (*Out of print.*)   ,,
168. Caxton's Ordre of Chyualry, ed. A. T. P. Byles. (*Out of print.*)   1925
169. The Southern Passion, ed. Beatrice Brown. (*Out of print.*)   ,,
170. Walton's Boethius, ed. M. Science. (*Out of print.*)   ,,
171. Pecock's Reule of Cristen Religioun, ed. W. C. Greet. (*Out of print.*)   1926
172. The Seege or Batayle of Troye, ed. M. E. Barnicle. (*Out of print.*)   ,,
173. Hawes' Pastime of Pleasure, ed. W. E. Mead. (*Out of print.*)   1927
174. The Life of St. Anne, ed. R. E. Parker. (*Out of print.*)   ,,
175. Barclay's Eclogues, ed. Beatrice White. (*Reprinted* 1961.) 35*s*.   ,,
176. Caxton's Prologues and Epilogues, ed. W. J. B. Crotch. (*Reprinted* 1956.) 45*s*.   ,,
177. Byrhtferth's Manual, ed. S. J. Crawford. (*Out of print.*)   1928
178. The Revelations of St. Birgitta, ed. W. P. Cumming. (*Out of print.*)   ,,
179. The Castell of Pleasure, ed. R. Cornelius. (*Out of print.*)   ,,
180. The Apologye of Syr Thomas More, ed. A. I. Taft. (*Out of print.*)   1929
181. The Dance of Death, ed. F. Warren. (*Out of print.*)   ,,
182. Speculum Christiani, ed. G. Holmstedt. (*Out of print.*)   ,,
183. The Northern Passion (Supplement), ed. W. Heuser and Frances Foster. (*Out of print.*)   1930
184. The Poems of John Audelay, ed. Ella K. Whiting. (*Out of print.*)   ,,
185. Lovelich's Merlin, ed. E. A. Kock. Part III. (*Out of print.*)   ,,
186. Harpsfield's Life of More, ed. Elsie V. Hitchcock and R. W. Chambers. (*Reprinted* 1963.) 45*s*.   1931
187. Whittinton and Stanbridge's Vulgaria, ed. B. White. (*Out of print.*)   ,,
188. The Siege of Jerusalem, ed. E. Kölbing and Mabel Day. 27*s*.   ,,
189. Caxton's Fayttes of Armes and of Chyualrye, ed. A. T. Byles. 37*s*. 6*d*.   1932
190. English Mediæval Lapidaries, ed. Joan Evans and Mary Serjeantson. (*Reprinted* 1960.) 20*s*.   ,,
191. The Seven Sages, ed. K. Brunner. (*Out of print.*)   ,,
191A.On the Continuity of English Prose, by R. W. Chambers. (*Reprinted* 1957.) 21*s*.   ,,
192. Lydgate's Minor Poems, ed. H. N. MacCracken. Part II, Secular Poems. (*Reprinted* 1961.) 40*s*.   1933
193. Seinte Marherete, re-ed. Frances Mack. (*Reprinted* 1958.) 45*s*.   ,,
194. The Exeter Book, Part II, ed. W. S. Mackie. (*Reprinted* 1958.) 37*s*. 6*d*.   ,,
195. The Quatrefoil of Love, ed. I. Gollancz and M. Weale. (*Out of print.*)   1934
196. A Short English Metrical Chronicle, ed. E. Zettl. (*Out of print.*)   ,,
197. Roper's Life of More, ed. Elsie V. Hitchcock. (*Reprinted* 1958.) 30*s*.   ,,
198. Firumbras and Otuel and Roland, ed. Mary O'Sullivan. (*Out of print.*)   ,,
199. Mum and the Sothsegger, ed. Mabel Day and R. Steele. 21*s*.   ,,
200. Speculum Sacerdotale, ed. E. H. Weatherly. (*Out of print.*)   1935
201. Knyghthode and Bataile, ed. R. Dyboski and Z. M. Arend. (*Out of print.*)   ,,
202. Palsgrave's Acolastus, ed. P. L. Carver. (*Out of print.*)   ,,
203. Amis and Amiloun, ed. MacEdward Leach. (*Reprinted* 1960.) 30*s*.   ,,
204. Valentine and Orson, ed. Arthur Dickson. (*Out of print.*)   1936
205. Tales from the Decameron, ed. H. G. Wright. (*Out of print.*)   ,,
206. Bokenham's Lives of Holy Women (Lives of the Saints), ed. Mary S. Serjeantson. (*Out of print.*)   ,,
207. Liber de Diversis Medicinis, ed. Margaret S. Ogden. (*Out of print.*)   ,,
208. The Parker Chronicle and Laws (facsimile), ed. R. Flower and A. H. Smith. 126*s*.   1937
209. Middle English Sermons from MS. Roy. 18 B. xxiii, ed. W. O. Ross. (*Reprinted* 1960.) 42*s*.   1938
210. Sir Gawain and the Green Knight, ed. I. Gollancz. With Introductory essays by Mabel Day and M. S. Serjeantson. (*Reprinted* 1964.) 15*s*.   ,,
211. Dictes and Sayings of the Philosophers, ed. C. F. Bühler. (*Reprinted* 1961.) 45*s*.   1939
212. The Book of Margery Kempe, Part I, ed. S. B. Meech and Hope Emily Allen. (*Reprinted* 1961.) 42*s*.   ,,
213. Ælfric's De Temporibus Anni, ed. H. Henel. (*Out of print.*)   1940
214. Morley's Translation of Boccaccio's De Claris Mulieribus, ed. H. G. Wright. (*Out of print.*)   ,,
215. English Poems of Charles of Orleans, Part I, ed. R. Steele. (*Out of print.*)   1941
216. The Latin Text of the Ancrene Riwle, ed. Charlotte D'Evelyn. (*Reprinted* 1957.) 45*s*.   ,,

The Original and Extra Series of the 'Early English Text Society'

217. Book of Vices and Virtues, ed. W. Nelson Francis. (*Out of print.*)		1942
218. The Cloud of Unknowing and the Book of Privy Counselling, ed. Phyllis Hodgson. (*Reprinted* 1958.) 40*s*.		1943
219. The French Text of the Ancrene Riwle, B.M. Cotton MS. Vitellius. F. VII, ed. J. A. Herbert. (*Out of print.*)		"
220. English Poems of Charles of Orleans, Part II, ed. R. Steele and Mabel Day. (*Out of print.*)		1944
221. Sir Degrevant, ed. L. F. Casson. (*Out of print.*)		"
222. Ro. Ba.'s Life of Syr Thomas More, ed. Elsie V. Hitchcock and Mgr. P. E. Hallett. (*Reprinted* 1957.) 52*s*. 6*d*.		1945
223. Tretyse of Loue, ed. J. H. Fisher. (*Out of print.*)		"
224. Athelston, ed. A. McI. Trounce. (*Reprinted* 1957.) 30*s*.		1946
225. The English Text of the Ancrene Riwle, B.M. Cotton MS. Nero A. XIV, ed. Mabel Day. (*Reprinted* 1957.) 35*s*.		"
226. Respublica, re-ed. W. W. Greg. (*Out of print.*)		"
227. Kyng Alisaunder, ed. G. V. Smithers. Vol. I, Text. (*Reprinted* 1961.) 45*s*.		1947
228. The Metrical Life of St. Robert of Knaresborough, ed. J. Bazire. (*Out of print.*)		"
229. The English Text of the Ancrene Riwle, Gonville and Caius College MS. 234/120, ed. R. M. Wilson. With Introduction by N. R. Ker. (*Reprinted* 1957.) 35*s*.		1948
230. The Life of St. George by Alexander Barclay, ed. W. Nelson. (*Reprinted* 1960.) 40*s*.		"
231. Deonise Hid Diuinite, and other treatises related to *The Cloud of Unknowing*, ed. Phyllis Hodgson. (*Reprinted* 1958.) 42*s*.		1949
232. The English Text of the Ancrene Riwle, B.M. Royal MS. 8 O. 1, ed. A. C. Baugh. (*Reprinted* 1958.) 30*s*.		"
233. The Bibliotheca Historica of Diodorus Siculus translated by John Skelton, ed. F. M. Salter and H. L. R. Edwards. Vol. I, Text. 63*s*.		1950
234. Caxton: Paris and Vienne, ed. MacEdward Leach. 40*s*.		1951
235. The South English Legendary, Corpus Christi College Cambridge MS. 145 and B.M. M.S. Harley 2277, &c., ed. Charlotte D'Evelyn and Anna J. Mill. Text, Vol. I. (*Out of print.*)		"
236. The South English Legendary. Text, Vol. II. (*Out of print.*)		1952
[E.S. 87. Two Coventry Corpus Christi Plays, re-ed. H. Craig. Second Edition. (*Out of print.*)]		"
237. Kyng Alisaunder, ed. G. V. Smithers. Vol. II, Introduction, Commentary, and Glossary. 50*s*.		1953
238. The Phonetic Writings of Robert Robinson, ed. E. J. Dobson. 40*s*.		"
239. The Bibliotheca Historica of Diodorus Siculus translated by John Skelton, ed. F. M. Salter and H. L. R. Edwards. Vol. II. Introduction, Notes, and Glossary. 25*s*.		1954
240. The French Text of the Ancrene Riwle, Trinity College, Cambridge, MS. R. 14. 7, ed. W. H. Trethewey. 55*s*.		"
241. Þe Wohunge of ure Lauerd, and other pieces, ed. W. Meredith Thompson. 45*s*.		1955
242. The Salisbury Psalter, ed. Celia Sisam and Kenneth Sisam. 90*s*.		1955–56
243. George Cavendish: The Life and Death of Cardinal Wolsey, ed. Richard S. Sylvester. (*Reprinted* 1961.) 45*s*.		1957
244. The South English Legendary. Vol. III, Introduction and Glossary, ed. Charlotte D'Evelyn. 30*s*.		"
245. Beowulf (facsimile). With Transliteration by J. Zupitza, new collotype plates, and Introduction by N. Davis. 84*s*.		1958
246. The Parlement of the Thre Ages, ed. M. Y. Offord. 40*s*.		1959
247. Facsimile of MS. Bodley 34 (Katherine Group). With Introduction by N. R. Ker. 50*s*.		"
248. Þe Liflade ant te Passiun of Seinte Iuliene, ed. S. R. T. O. d'Ardenne. 40*s*.		1960
249. Ancrene Wisse, Corpus Christi College, Cambridge, MS. 402, ed. J. R. R. Tolkien. With an Introduction by N. R. Ker. 40*s*.		"
250. Laȝamon's Brut, ed. G. L. Brook and R. F. Leslie. Vol. I, Text (first part). 80*s*.		1961
251. Facsimile of the Cotton and Jesus Manuscripts of the Owl and the Nightingale. With Introduction by N. R. Ker. 42*s*.		1962
252. The English Text of the Ancrene Riwle, B.M. Cotton MS. Titus D. XVIII, ed. Frances M. Mack, and Lanhydrock Fragment, ed. A. Zettersten. 40*s*.		"
253. The Bodley Version of Mandeville's Travels, ed. M. C. Seymour. 40*s*.		1963
254. Ywain and Gawain, ed. Albert B. Friedman and Norman T. Harrington. 40*s*.		"
255. Facsimile of B.M. MS. Harley 2253 (The Harley Lyrics). With Introduction by N. R. Ker. 84*s*.		1964
256. Sir Eglamour of Artois, ed. Frances E. Richardson. 40*s*.		1965
257. Sir Thomas Chaloner: The Praise of Folie, ed. Clarence H. Miller. 42*s*.		"

The following is a select list of forthcoming volumes. Other texts are under consideration:

258. The Orchard of Syon, ed. Phyllis Hodgson and Gabriel M. Liegey. Vol. I, Text. (*At press.*) 84*s*.		1966
259. Uncollected Homilies of Ælfric, ed. J. C. Pope. Vol. I. (*At press.*) 84*s*.		1967
260. Uncollected Homilies of Ælfric, ed. J. C. Pope. Vol. II. (*At press.*) 84*s*.		1968

Guy de Chauliac's Chirurgia Magna, ed. Margaret S. Ogden.
Libeaus Desconus, ed. M. Mills.
Laȝamon's Brut, ed. G. L. Brook and R. F. Leslie, Vols. II and III.
Ælfric: Catholic Homilies, First Series, ed. P. Clemoes.
The Paston Letters, ed. N. Davis.
The English Text of the Ancrene Riwle, edited from all the extant manuscripts:
    Bodleian MS. Vernon, ed. G. V. Smithers.
    B.M. Cotton MS. Cleopatra C. VI, ed. E. J. Dobson.
    Magdalene College, Cambridge, MS. Pepys 2498, ed. A. Zettersten.
The York Plays, re-ed. Arthur Brown.
The Macro Plays, re-ed. Mark Eccles.
The Cely Letters, ed. A. H. Hanham.

March 1965

Publisher
LONDON: THE OXFORD UNIVERSITY PRESS, AMEN HOUSE, E.C. 4

The manufacturer's authorised representative in the EU for product safety is Oxford University Press España S.A. of El Parque Empresarial San Fernando de Henares, Avenida de Castilla, 2 - 28830 Madrid (www.oup.es/en or product.safety@oup.com). OUP España S.A. also acts as importer into Spain of products made by the manufacturer.
Printed and bound by CPI Group (UK) Ltd, Croydon, CR0 4YY

20/03/2026

02075341-0001